Water Bath Canning & Preserving for Beginners

A Step-By-Step Guide to Start Your Own Preservative-Free Prepper Pantry - Featuring 55 Starter Recipes to Can Fruits, Vegetables, Jams, Sauces, and More

Elizabeth Ash

© Copyright 2022 - All rights reserved.

The content contained within this book may not be reproduced, duplicated or transmitted without direct written permission from the author or the publisher.

Under no circumstances will any blame or legal responsibility be held against the publisher, or author, for any damages, reparation, or monetary loss due to the information contained within this book, either directly or indirectly.

Legal Notice:

This book is copyright protected. It is only for personal use. You cannot amend, distribute, sell, use, quote or paraphrase any part, or the content within this book, without the consent of the author or publisher.

Disclaimer Notice:

Please note the information contained within this document is for educational and entertainment purposes only. All effort has been executed to present accurate, up to date, reliable, complete information. No warranties of any kind are declared or implied. Readers acknowledge that the author is not engaged in the rendering of legal, financial, medical or professional advice. The content within this book has been derived from various sources. Please consult a licensed professional before attempting any techniques outlined in this book.

By reading this document, the reader agrees that under no circumstances is the author responsible for any losses, direct or indirect, that are incurred as a result of the use of the information contained within this document, including, but not limited to, errors, omissions, or inaccuracies.

Table of Contents

INTRODUCTION: THE WONDERS OF WATER BATH CANNING 1

CHAPTER 1: WATER BATH CANNING BASICS 5

   HOW DOES WATER BATH CANNING WORK? 6
   HOW DOES WATER BATH CANNING DIFFER FROM OTHER FOOD PRESERVATION METHODS 7
      Water Bath Canning 7
      Atmospheric Steam Canning 8
      Pressure Canning 8
   BENEFITS OF WATER BATH CANNING 9
      It's a Very Simple and Safe Procedure 9
      Eliminates Bacteria That Causes Food Spoilage 9
      Allows You to Preserve Certain Low-Acid Foods Through Proper Processing 10
      Creates a Vacuum Inside the Jars to Keep the Contents Preserved 10
      Ensures a Long Shelf-Life 11
   POSSIBLE RISKS OF WATER BATH CANNING 11
      Contamination Through Unsterilized Tools 11
      Reusing Old Lids 11
      The Danger of Improperly Canning Low-Acid Foods 12
      Botulism 12

CHAPTER 2: BEST AND WORST FOODS TO PRESERVE THROUGH WATER BATH CANNING 15

   THE BEST FOODS TO PRESERVE 15
      Fruits 16
      Jams and Jellies 16
      Pickled or Fermented Foods 17
      Relishes, Chutneys, Pie Fillings, Juices, and More 17
      Salsas and Sauces 17
      Tomatoes 17
      Vegetables 18
   THE WORST FOODS TO PRESERVE (AND WHY) 18
      Meat, Poultry, and Seafood 19
      Most Types of Veggies 19
      Soup 20
      Vegetable, Meat, Poultry, or Seafood Stock 20
      Dairy Products 20

CHAPTER 3: HOW TO START 21

   BASIC EQUIPMENT NEEDED 21
      Pot 22
      Canning Jars 22
      Canning Lids 23
      Rings 23
      Canning Rack 23

  Other Tools and Equipment 23
 GETTING STARTED WITH WATER BATH CANNING 24
  Plan Before You Process 24
  Read the Recipe Carefully Before You Start 24
  Sterilize the Jars, but Not the Lids 25
  Fill the Pot With Enough Water 25
  Know the Basic Water Bath Canning Steps 25
  Make Sure There is Enough Headspace 26
  Take Note of Processing Times and Altitudes 27
  Take Note of the Differences Between Raw and Hot Pack Preservation 27
  Use New Lids Each Time You Process and Remove the Rings Before Storage 28
  Make Sure That the Jars are Sealed Properly 28
  Label and Store the Jars Properly 28
  Wash All of Your Tools and Equipment After Use 29
  Never Make Up Your Own Canning Recipes 29

CHAPTER 4: PREPARING YOUR PREPPER PANTRY 31

 THE BENEFITS OF HAVING A PREPPER PANTRY 31
  Food Security 32
  Peace of Mind 32
  Convenience 33
  Customization 33
 TIPS FOR PLANNING YOUR PREPPER PANTRY 33
  Create a Plan 33
  Determine the Location of Your Prepper Pantry 34
  Build Your Prepper Pantry Gradually 34
  Come Up With a Budget 34
  Focus on Nutrition and Variety 35
  Rotate Your Stocks 35
  Start Meal Planning 36
 ALL ABOUT MEAL PLANNING AND HOW TO START 36

CHAPTER 5: RECIPES FOR CANNING FRUITS 39

 APRICOTS 39
 BLACKBERRIES 40
 CHERRIES 43
 CRANBERRIES 44
 FRUIT COCKTAIL 46
 GRAPES 47
 KIWI 49
 LEMONS 50
 MANGO 52
 PEACHES 53
 PEARS 55
 PLUMS 56
 RASPBERRIES 57

CHAPTER 6: RECIPES FOR CANNING VEGETABLES 61

 CANDIED JALAPEÑOS 61
 DILL PICKLES 62

 Mushrooms 64
 Pickled Asparagus 66
 Pickled Beets 68
 Pickled Carrots 70
 Pickled Eggplants 72
 Pickled Green Beans 73
 Pickled Mixed Veggies 75
 Pickled Onions 76
 Spicy Pickled Garlic 78
 Tomatoes 79

CHAPTER 7: RECIPES FOR CANNING JAMS AND JELLIES 83
 3-Berry Jam 83
 Coconut and Pineapple Jam 84
 Orange and Fig Jam 86
 Salted Cantaloupe Jam 87
 Zucchini Jam 89
 Corn Cob Jelly 91
 Dandelion Jelly 92
 Mint Jelly 94
 Spicy Pepper Jelly 96
 Watermelon Jelly 98

CHAPTER 8: RECIPES FOR CANNING SALSAS AND SAUCES 101
 Apple and Peach Salsa 101
 Classic Tomato Salsa 103
 Roasted Spicy Salsa 105
 Salsa Verde 107
 Sweet Strawberry Salsa 109
 Barbeque Sauce 111
 Chocolate and Raspberry Sauce 114
 Pear Sauce with Vanilla and Caramel 115
 Pizza Sauce 117
 Spicy Pepper Sauce 119

CHAPTER 9: OTHER CANNING RECIPES TO TRY 121
 Ketchup 121
 Wholegrain Mustard 123
 Pickle Relish 125
 Sweet Corn Relish 126
 Apple Pie Filling 129
 Sweet Pecan Pie Filling 131
 Date and Banana Chutney 132
 Green Tomato Chutney 134
 Vegetable Juice 136
 Sauerkraut 137

CHAPTER 10: FOCUSING ON SAFETY 141
 Common Water Bath Canning Mistakes to Avoid 141
  Not Starting With High-Quality Ingredients *141*

Using a Water Bath Canner for Foods That Need to Be Pressure Canned 141
Using the Wrong Size of Canning Jars 142
Using Damaged Canning Jars 142
Removing Air Bubbles With a Metal Spoon 142
Not Adding Enough Water to the Pot 142
Not Considering Your Altitude 143
Taking the Jars Out of the Canner Right After Processing 143
Storing the Jars Without Removing the Rings 143
Not Labeling Your Jars 144
Essential Safety Tips to Keep in Mind 144

CONCLUSION: WATER BATH CANNING LIKE A PRO 147

REFERENCES 149
Image References 155

Introduction:

The Wonders of Water Bath Canning

Have you ever seen a prepper pantry?

You know, one of those storage spaces that is filled with cans, bottles, and boxes of preserved food and other essential items. Having such a room at home will make you feel more confident about your safety in case something unexpected occurs.

Building your own prepper pantry might seem like an overwhelming task, but it doesn't have to be. As long as you have extra space in your home, you can start filling it with essential items.

These days, there is a lot of uncertainty. The world is constantly changing and we constantly hear devastating news about natural disasters and other unexpected tragedies. Such news often comes with feelings of fear, especially if you know that you aren't ready to deal with situations like those. Some of the most common worrisome thoughts that may have gone through your mind include:

- That the food you have at home will go bad, thus rendering it inedible.
- Power outages that last for a long time will cause your stocked freezer meals and other frozen products to go bad.
- All the money you have spent on food will go to waste.
- There will be food shortages, which means that you won't even get a chance to buy food even if you have the money for it.
- The only foods available will contain a lot of chemicals and preservatives, and eating too much of these could contribute to the development of health issues.

When you're already struggling in the midst of a natural disaster, having to deal with these things will make life even more difficult for you. Fortunately, you can easily calm your mind by starting to build your own prepper pantry. Stock your pantry with healthy, tasty foods that you have made yourself. Preserving your own foods at home is highly recommended when building a prepper pantry. And when it comes to preserving food, one of the easiest and most wonderful ways to do this is through water bath canning.

Water bath canning is a type of preservation method. The process involves canning high-acid foods in glass jars. This is a very easy process where you fill jars with food, seal them with lids, then boil the jars for specific amounts of time in order to maintain the quality of the food stored inside. It's such a simple process that you can easily do it at home. High-acid foods include fruits, jellies, jams, relishes, pickled vegetables, and more.

If you have never tried home canning before, it's recommended to start with water bath canning because of the simplicity of the process. When I became interested in food preservation, I started with this process too.

I learned all about water canning through my grandmother. In fact, I learned all about food preservation and building a prepper pantry from my grandmother too. Whenever I visited her home, I was fascinated with this one room where she kept different kinds of food. When I was young, I used to sneak into that room often just to stare at all the jars and bottles.

As I grew older, my grandmother introduced me to the importance of having food stores at home. At first, I didn't really take her seriously. But then, the more I thought about it, the more I realized that having a prepper pantry made a lot of sense. So my husband and I started learning more about it. We started with water bath canning as this process was something my grandmother had been doing since she was young.

When she found out that we wanted to preserve our own food, she passed down her secrets to us. Since then, we have been canning our own food at home. Now, we have a fully-stocked prepper pantry that keeps us feeling safe, food-wise even if something unexpected were to happen. We have gotten so good at preserving different kinds of food that we even give them out as gifts, which always brings a smile to the faces of our friends and loved ones.

To take things even further, we have decided to write this book to share what we know about water bath canning with anyone who is interested. The great thing about this process is that it's one of the most popular and easiest ways to preserve different types of food. Water bath canning is an easy process, which you can master given the right knowledge. And you don't even need any special equipment for it.

Water bath canning is recommended by modern homesteaders because of its convenience and simplicity. Once you master this process, then you can start learning how to preserve food through other processes too. Although this process might seem intimidating, especially if you haven't tried home canning before, you don't have to worry.

From defining the process, explaining how it works, and what are the benefits you can gain from it, there is much for you to learn. By the end of this book, you will have a thorough understanding of what water bath canning is all about. You can even start canning foods at home since this book also contains lots of recipes to get you started. So if you're ready to start learning, turn the page, and let's begin!

Chapter 1:

Water Bath Canning Basics

Simply put, water bath canning is a process where you preserve food by placing it into a jar, then immersing it in a hot water bath. It's important to place the food in hot jars that you have already sterilized. Placing the jars in boiling water kills off the bacteria that cause foods to spoil. This process also sucks out the air from inside the jars, which then allows the lids to seal the jars tightly. This is important so that the food inside the jars stays shelf-stable.

One of the best things about water bath canning is that it's a very simple process. You can invest in a water bath canner, but a large stockpot would work just as well. As long as you know how the process works, you will be able to preserve many types of food through water bath canning.

How Does Water Bath Canning Work?

Simple as this process is, it's very good at preserving certain types of food. Water bath canning is so effective because it kills bacteria and sucks out the air from the jars to prevent the growth of new bacteria. Both processes prevent the food inside the jars from getting spoiled. The process works this way:

- You preheat your water bath canner with the jars inside in order to sterilize them. You can sterilize the jars separately too.
- After sterilizing the jars, you pack the food inside along with any liquid you would use to preserve the food.
- Once you immerse the jars inside the water bath canner, the high temperature of the water sucks out the air from the foods and the jar itself.
- A vacuum is created inside the jar, which then causes the lid to seal the jars tightly.

You must make sure that the rims and lids are very clean before you place the jars in the canner. Do this by using a paper towel to wipe the rims before screwing the lids on tightly. Water bath canning is only suitable for high-acid foods. It's also possible to can low-acid foods, but you need to acidify them first through pickling or some other safe process. If you plan to do this, it's important for you to follow the recipes carefully to ensure that you preserve the foods safely.

If you want to start preserving foods through water bath canning, you don't need a specialized canning pot for this purpose. You can use any stockpot that's big and deep enough to place your jars. It's also important for the canner (or pot) to have a lid to ensure that the water inside the pot boils continuously throughout the processing time.

Once in a while, the jars might break while you are processing them inside the canner. If this happens, gently take the broken jars out of the canner along with the contents. At this point, you can continue processing the other jars. As for the broken jars, discard them along with all of their contents.

How Does Water Bath Canning Differ From Other Food Preservation Methods

Water bath canning isn't the only food preservation method out there. But since it's the easiest, it's recommended to start with this one. To help you understand this process better, let's take a look at the different methods of canning. This will also help you understand what sets water bath canning apart from the other processes.

Water Bath Canning

For this process, the jars placed inside the water bath canner are surrounded by boiling water. To ensure that the process works correctly, you need to make sure that the canner contains enough boiling water to surround the jars completely. You also need to place a rack inside the pot rather than placing the jars directly into the bottom of the pot. This allows water to circulate underneath the jars while processing.

There should also be enough space on top of the pot to ensure that the water level is at least two inches above the jars. You can either purchase a water bath canner and think of it as an investment or you can work with a pot that you already have at home, at least at the beginning. Just make sure that the pot is big enough for the jars you will process. For instance, if your pot is a bit small, you need to buy jars that are a bit small too. That way, they can fit inside the pot for proper processing.

Water bath canning is suitable for most types of fruits, jams, jellies, pickles, and other high-acid foods. Simplicity is one of the features that sets this process apart, which is why it's perfect for those who want to learn how to preserve foods through canning without any previous experience. It's also ideal because you don't need to have special equipment in order to start canning your own food at home.

Atmospheric Steam Canning

This is a recently developed canning method that can be used for food preservation at home. For this, you will need an atmospheric steam canner. This process is also suitable for high-acid foods. Atmospheric steam canners have a low base, a tall lid, and a rack for placing the jars. The lid has a special design with holes near the base. The holes allow the steam to escape during the canning process.

When processing jars with food in this type of canner, you need to keep the lid on throughout the process. Since an atmospheric steam canner works the same way as a water bath canner, processing times are usually the same. However, if you need to process foods for more than 45 minutes, you shouldn't use this process as the water in the canner might evaporate completely before reaching the proper processing time.

Pressure Canning

Pressure canning is the only suitable method for canning low-acid foods like most vegetables, meat, poultry, seafood, and more. This is the only safe method for canning such foods that doesn't pose a risk of botulism. Since botulism spores can survive temperatures as high as the boiling point of water, canning low-acid foods using steam or water bath canners isn't safe. Pressure canning is your only option.

While processing, the temperature inside a pressure canner gets high enough to eliminate botulism spores, thus making the preserved food safe enough to eat. For this method, you need a pressure canner. This is a specialized piece of equipment, unlike the simple pot that you would need for water bath canning. You need to invest in a pressure canner if you want to preserve your foods using this method. Since it's possible to preserve many other types of food using the water bath canning method, many choose to start with the simple process.

Apart from these three canning methods, there are other methods used a long time ago. Unfortunately, these methods aren't considered safe anymore. Thesy include:

- Using an oven to process jars. This isn't recommended because it may cause the jars to explode. Even if they remain intact, ovens won't heat the contents of the jars evenly to ensure proper preservation.
- The hot fill or open kettle method where you simply pour hot food into empty jars, then screw the lids immediately. Since the contents of the jars are hot, the heat seals the lids in place. However, this method isn't safe because it doesn't produce enough heat to prevent the contents of the jars from spoiling.
- Some even try canning using dishwashers, slow cookers, microwaves, or crock pots, all of which aren't recommended because of the same reasons as above.

Aside from these methods, it also isn't recommended to use canning chemicals or powders that are supposed to replace the heating process. Canning foods for preservation is a sensitive process that can produce unsafe results if not done correctly, so it's important to only stick with proper canning methods.

Benefits of Water Bath Canning

Many modern homesteaders have started preserving foods through water bath canning. This has become a very popular method of canning that will allow you to fill your prepper pantry with healthy, delicious foods. If you're still wondering why you should go with this method, take a look at the many benefits you can look forward to.

It's a Very Simple and Safe Procedure

One of the best benefits of water bath canning is its simplicity. Anyone with a big enough pot at home can do this process. As you will discover later, the recipes for canning foods this way are very easy to do. As long as you follow the steps and processing times correctly, you can produce safely preserved foods to add to your stockpile.

Eliminates Bacteria That Causes Food Spoilage

Although water bath canning won't eliminate botulism spores, it's effective enough to destroy other bacteria that can cause food spoilage. These include Listeria monocytogenesm, Salmonella enterica, Escherichia coli O157:H7, and more. Again, you can only gain this benefit if you make sure to follow the proper water bath canning procedures, both for high-acid foods and for low-acid foods that you cook or process first before preserving them in your water bath canner.

Allows You to Preserve Certain Low-Acid Foods Through Proper Processing

Speaking of low-acid foods, you can preserve some of these too. But before doing this, you need to either cook the foods first or pickle them, such as in the case of most vegetables. After cooking, processing the foods inside the jars through water bath canning further drives acids into the foods. This, in turn, strengthens the preservation process, which makes even low-acid foods safe for long-term storage.

Creates a Vacuum Inside the Jars to Keep the Contents Preserved

Over time, oxygen causes the degradation of food in terms of nutrition, appearance, and flavor. This is a process that occurs naturally when foods are exposed to oxygen. Since water bath canning sucks out the air from the jars and the foods themselves, it creates a vacuum inside the jars to preserve the contents. When this happens, the lids seal the jars tightly, which prevents air from re-entering the jars until you open them for consumption.

Ensures a Long Shelf-Life

Since water bath canning preserves the contents of the jars, you can store them for months or even years after processing. This long shelf-life is very important, especially if you're planning to build a prepper pantry at home.

Since water bath canning allows you to preserve fresh ingredients without using unnecessary or artificial ingredients, this process also contributes to a healthier lifestyle. You won't have to rely on processed foods just because they have longer shelf lives. You can start preserving your own fresh, nutritious ingredients to ensure that you can keep eating healthy foods even when disaster strikes.

Possible Risks of Water Bath Canning

Although preserving food through a water bath canner is generally safe and simple, it isn't a perfect process. In fact, it can be quite risky if you don't learn how to can foods properly. This is why educating yourself about the process is of the essence. To help you understand everything about water bath canning, let's go through the possible risks that you should look out for.

Contamination Through Unsterilized Tools

One of the biggest risks of water bath canning is contamination. If you don't sterilize the jars and any other tools or equipment you use, you could compromise the safety of the food you preserve. Even if you process the jars correctly, using contaminated tools could result in unsafe outcomes. This is why one of the first steps in any recipe for water bath canning is to sterilize your jars first. This is essential to minimize the risk of bacterial growth or contamination through toxins.

It's not enough to simply wash the jars; you should sterilize them in boiling water for a minimum of 10 minutes. Make sure that all of the tools you use for preparing and cooking the ingredients are clean too. Cleanliness prevents contamination, which ensures the safety of your final products.

Reusing Old Lids

It's possible to reuse canning jars, lids, and rings to store food. But when it comes to canning, it's important to purchase new lids. New lids include rubber rings and they are only suitable for one use when it comes to canning. Reusing lids isn't safe as there is a very big chance that they won't seal properly, which means that the food inside won't be preserved safely. To avoid this, you should mark the lids of your jars before storing them. That way, you know which lids have already been processed in the water bath canner. Use these for short-term storage of foods.

The Danger of Improperly Canning Low-Acid Foods

In this book, you will find many recipes for preserving foods using a water bath canner. If you have tried all of the recipes in this book and you want to try canning other foods, make sure to find recipes that are meant for water bath canning. This is especially important for low-acid foods. While it's possible to preserve some types of low-acid foods in a water bath canner, you need to follow the correct process to ensure your safety. Also, take note of the foods that can only be canned through a pressure canner. We'll go through these foods in the next chapter.

Botulism

This is the most dangerous risk that could come from water bath canning. If you know how to use your water bath canner properly and you apply your knowledge, there is minimal to no risk of botulism. However, if you don't learn how to preserve food through water bath canning properly, this is one risk that could prove fatal.

The bacteria known as Clostridium botulinum causes botulism. This bacteria can be found in improperly preserved canned or jarred goods. Clostridium botulinum produces toxins that attack your nervous system, causing paralysis or even death. Botulism occurs when preserved foods aren't properly processed or sealed.

The bacteria cannot survive in foods with high acid levels, which is why it's perfectly safe to preserve these types of foods through water bath canning. In order to preserve low-acid foods in the same way, you may need to add lemon juice, vinegar, or some other type of acid to increase the level of acidity and eliminate the risk of botulism. This is why you need to pickle vegetables first before canning them using the water bath method.

Apart from being aware of the potential risks of water bath canning, you should also know how to spot issues after you have processed your food through this method. Do this by testing the lids of the jars after they have cooled down completely. Also, make sure that there are no cracks in any of the jars as these could cause contamination.

When it's time to open the jars so you can consume the contents, make sure that the lids make a popping noise when you unscrew them. If they don't, it's better to discard the jar and its contents. Finally, check the underside of the lids to make sure that there aren't any molds, foam, or any odd liquid on them. If you smell something stinky or moldy after opening the jar, discard it along with all the contents. Keeping all of these things in mind will ensure that you will always be safe when processing and consuming your preserved foods.

Chapter 2:

Best and Worst Foods to Preserve Through Water Bath Canning

Deciding to create your own prepper pantry at home is a very smart move, especially with all the uncertainties of our world today. Even if nothing bad happens, you will still have peace of mind knowing that food-wise you're ready for anything. Also, you have the option to enjoy the foods you have preserved whenever you want. Then you can simply replace the jars you opened since you already know how the water bath canning process works.

But before you start canning foods at home, you should know which foods you can preserve through this process and which foods to avoid. Once you have this knowledge, you can start planning your ingredients before you visit your local farmer's market.

The Best Foods to Preserve

If it's your first time preserving foods through water bath canning, trying to learn everything you need to know can get quite overwhelming. But if you focus on one aspect of this process at a time, learning becomes much easier. After understanding how the process works, it's time to know which foods you can and cannot preserve through water bath canning. First, let's start with the high-acid foods that can be preserved through this method.

Fruits

Most types of fruits can be processed safely using a water bath. These include citrus fruits, apples, pears, plums, peaches, cherries, berries, and more. It's particularly beneficial to can seasonal fruits so that you can enjoy them all year round. Of course, you can also can the more common fruits just to make sure that you have them in your pantry even if something unexpected happens.

Jams and Jellies

Fruits and vegetables can be made into jams, jellies, preserves, and marmalades so that you can process them through water bath canning. It's easy to do this with high-acid fruits like oranges, berries, pears, and peaches, but you can also do this with low-acid fruits and vegetables. The key here is to add some acid to the mix before cooking them into jams and jellies. If you're not yet sure about canning raw ingredients, you can start with jams and jellies. These are much easier to preserve and they tend to have a longer shelf life. These preserved food items are so delicious, especially when you start with fresh ingredients when making them.

Pickled or Fermented Foods

If you want to stock your pantry with foods that don't contain a lot of sugar, such as jams and jellies, consider making pickled or fermented foods instead. Pickling and fermenting are highly recommended for low-acid vegetables. As you will discover, pickling recipes include a lot of vinegar, which significantly increases the acid content of the foods. The great thing about pickling is that it allows you to preserve many different types of veggies.

Relishes, Chutneys, Pie Fillings, Juices, and More

Relishes and chutneys also contain some type of a high-acid component such as vinegar, citric acid, or lemon juice. This addition allows you to process even low-acid ingredients using your water bath canner. Having relishes and chutneys at home allows you to pair these tasty treats with your meals.

If you have a sweet tooth or you enjoy baking a lot, consider making your own pie filling and juices using fresh ingredients. Having stocks of pie fillings allows you to make pies for yourself, your family, and even unexpected guests quickly. As for juices, there is nothing more refreshing than drinking juice made from real fruits and vegetables. It's also possible to preserve homemade condiments and dressings like ketchup, mustard, and vinaigrettes using your water bath canner.

Salsas and Sauces

Salsas and sauces are also considered high-acid foods because you will be adding components to them that are high in acid. These components make them suitable for water bath canning. Just make sure to use natural ingredients instead of artificial chemicals to ensure that the final product will always be healthy and of high quality.

Tomatoes

Technically, a tomato is a fruit even though it's often treated as a vegetable in cooking. It's possible to can whole tomatoes or use them as the main ingredient for salsa, juice, sauce, and more.

Vegetables

Some types of vegetables such as rhubarb can also be canned through this method. However, most types of vegetables need to undergo pickling or fermenting first before they can safely be processed. When it comes to veggies, you should always make sure that the recipe indicates that it is suitable for water bath canning, not pressure canning.

When it comes to adding more acid to low-acid ingredients, the key here is to find the right balance. Adding enough acid prevents the food from getting spoiled. Pay attention to the kind of acid you should add along with the quantity. This is very important, especially since water bath canning doesn't reach high enough temperatures during the canning process.

The Worst Foods to Preserve (and Why)

You have already learned how low-acid foods cannot be processed through water bath canning because this method doesn't reach temperatures that are high enough to destroy botulism and other types of bacteria. Although you can process some types of low-acid foods by adding acidic components, there are certain foods that shouldn't be preserved through water bath canning because of safety issues. Let's go through these foods now.

Meat, Poultry, and Seafood

Meat, poultry, and seafood can only be safely preserved using a pressure canner. Under no circumstances should you water bath can these protein sources. These foods don't contain enough acid, which means that they need to be processed at a very high temperature before being sealed. This eliminates the risk of bacteria growth and food spoilage.

Pressure canners can reach up to 240 °F, which is high enough for both raw and cooked meat, poultry, and seafood. You can even make stews and other ready-to-eat meals using these ingredients, then preserve them through pressure canning.

Most Types of Veggies

While it's possible to preserve some types of high-acid vegetables, most types of fresh veggies can't be safely processed using a water bath. Some examples of vegetables that shouldn't be processed through water bath canning include green beans, carrots, asparagus, leafy greens, and so much more. If you really want to preserve these vegetables, you need to pickle or ferment them first in order to make them suitable for processing.

Soup

Although it would be very convenient to can soup and store it in your prepper pantry, you don't have the option to do this if you will only preserve foods through water bath canning. Just like veggies, soups usually contain ingredients that are low in acid. Once you have mastered water bath canning, you may think about moving on to pressure canning if you want to expand your stockpile even further.

Vegetable, Meat, Poultry, or Seafood Stock

In order to make stock, you would have to boil either vegetables, meat, or poultry in water for a long time along with some other ingredients to season the broth. However, the end product doesn't contain enough acid for it to be safely processed through water bath canning. This method won't heat up the contents of the jars enough to destroy all bacteria that may grow or thrive in the liquid.

Dairy Products

In general, dairy products cannot be preserved using any kind of canning method. To preserve dairy products, you need to freeze-dry them. They are also low in acid and when they reach room temperature, botulism spores can grow and thrive in these foods. Therefore, you should try to avoid using these foods in pie fillings, soups, and other recipes that you plan to process through canning.

When it comes to determining the foods that shouldn't be preserved through water bath canning, check the acid levels. If you plan to search for recipes online after trying all of the recipes here, make sure that those recipes are specifically meant for water bath canning. Do this to make sure that you can eat the food you preserve at home.

Chapter 3:

How to Start

Water bath canning is a simple process, but that doesn't mean that you can do it however you want. To preserve your foods safely, you need to follow recipes and processing times carefully. Since you will essentially try to lengthen the shelf life of various foods in order to keep them in your pantry, safety is of the essence. To help you get started, let's go through the fundamentals of water bath canning from the equipment you need to some practical tips to get you started.

Basic Equipment Needed

Although you don't need any special equipment for water bath canning, you do need to prepare a number of items to start preserving your food at home. You may already have some of these items at home. If not, you can easily find them in shops that offer various kitchenware.

Pot

First, you need a large, sturdy pot that comes with a tight-fitting lid. The pot should be deep enough to hold the jars while having space above and below. Remember that you will place a rack inside the pot so that the water will boil underneath the jars. There should also be space above the jars as they need to be completely submerged in water during the water bath canning process. You can even use a Dutch oven for this purpose if you have one that is deep enough.

Canning Jars

You also need canning jars made of glass to put your food into. Purchase jars that are specifically meant for canning as these are the ones that come with proper lids and rings. It's not recommended to simply use old pickle or mayonnaise jars even if they are made of glass. Since this is where you will store your food, it's important to invest in the right types of jars that will keep your preserved foods safe.

Canning Lids

When you buy canning jars, they should already come with proper lids. Just remember that lids should only be used once for canning. Although you can reuse the jars, you need to buy new lids each time you need to process new foods for preservation.

When purchasing new lids, make sure that they will fit the jars you have at home. This ensures that the jars will be sealed tightly and keep the contents safe. After using the lids once, you can reuse them for covering jars for short-term storage or non-food storage. If you don't plan to use them anymore, you can simply discard the used lids.

Rings

Also known as bands, the rings are supposed to screw over the top of the canning jars. They are meant to hold the lids in place while you are processing the jars and their contents. After processing and cooling down the jars, remove the rings, then check to see if the lids are sealed properly. It's important to remove the rings to prevent rust from forming on the lids. Unlike canning lids, rings can be reused, as long as they still fit securely over the lids that you buy and they don't have any kind of flaw or damage.

Canning Rack

A canning rack is a rack that you place inside the canner or stockpot. This is where you place the jars during the canning process. The rack is an important part of the whole setup as it prevents the jars from being in direct contact with the bottom of the pot. It reduces the risk of the jars breaking as it keeps the jars away from the heat of the stove underneath the pot. The rack also ensures that the jars are completely immersed in boiling water throughout the processing period.

If you will invest in a canner, it should already come with a canning rack. But if you will use a stockpot that you already have at home, you may purchase a round wire rack that fits snugly in the bottom of your pot.

Other Tools and Equipment

The items mentioned above are all of the basic items you need for your water bath canning journey. Now, let's go through some other items that aren't really required, but would make the process a lot easier:

- A canning funnel would make it easier for you to fill the jars without making a mess. This is particularly useful if you won't be using wide-mouthed jars.

- A flexible plastic or rubber spatula that you can use to release air bubbles that get into the jars before processing them in the water bath.

- A measuring stick that you can use to measure the headspace of each jar before screwing on the lid. You can also use this tool to remove air bubbles that may have entered the jars while you were filling them up.

- A bubble remover is the actual tool that you would use to remove the air bubbles from inside the jars.

- A jar lifter that you can use to take the jars out of the water bath and transfer them to the place where you will allow them to cool down. You may use a pair of tongs for this purpose, but a jar lifter is much easier and safer to use.

- Cloth kitchen towels where you will place the jars after processing. You need to allow the jars to cool down undisturbed on a flat surface before storing them.

By preparing all of these items, you will be ready to start preserving different types of food to store in your prepper pantry.

Getting Started with Water Bath Canning

After preparing all of the equipment you need, you should also start preparing yourself. Once you begin the process of water bath canning, it would be better if you are already familiar with all of the steps. That way, you can follow the recipe smoothly without having to stop frequently to remind yourself of the steps you need to take. Here are some tips and steps for you.

Plan Before You Process

If you are planning to stock your prepper pantry with food that you have preserved through water bath canning, you may want to practice meal planning too. This is a simple process wherein you plan your meals—or in this case, your food stocks—beforehand. Planning is an important first step so that you can buy just the right amount of ingredients needed for preservation.

Read the Recipe Carefully Before You Start

As a beginner, you should follow water bath canning recipes to ensure the best and safest results. As part of your planning process, you should also read the recipes carefully beforehand. This allows you to prepare the ingredients you need while making you familiar with all the steps you need to take throughout the water bath canning process. Familiarize yourself with the ingredients, the processing times, and the steps.

It's important to only follow recipes that have been tried and tested specifically for water bath canning. Remember that water bath canning isn't suitable for all types of foods. So if the recipe doesn't specify that you can use a water bath canner for it, find another one. The good news is that this book contains more than enough recipes for you to start with; all you have to do is read them carefully before you start.

Sterilize the Jars, but Not the Lids

It's important to sterilize the canning jars before you pack them with food. This is a very important step as it ensures that the jars are completely clean before use. You don't need to sterilize the lids, but you do need to wash them thoroughly.

After washing the lids and sterilizing the jars, make sure that they are completely dry before filling them. Any moisture could cause the contents to get spoiled. You don't need to sterilize the rings either because they won't touch the contents of the jars. It's also important to check the rims of the jars to ensure that they are free of nicks or chips. These types of damage could cause the jars to be sealed improperly.

Fill the Pot With Enough Water

When it's time to heat up your pot, place the wire rack inside it first. Then fill the pot with water making sure that there is enough to cover the jars by at least two inches. The longer the processing time is, the more water should be added. If you aren't sure, you may want to have another pot filled with boiling water on standby while you process. That way, you can keep adding water to the canner to ensure that the water level doesn't go down while processing. You may also mix a couple of tablespoons of white vinegar in the water. Although this isn't a requirement, it will prevent the outside of the jars from getting cloudy.

Know the Basic Water Bath Canning Steps

Although preparing the ingredients to fill the jars requires different steps, the steps for the actual canning process are all the same. Here are the steps:

- Prepare all of the ingredients you need.

- Heat up the water in your canner. You may sterilize the jars here, then take them out and dry them before filling.

- When you're almost ready with the jars and the contents, bring the pot to a gentle boil.

- After filling the jars, screw on the lids, and add the rings. At this point, the jars should be hot so they don't crack due to the sudden change in temperature.

- Place the jars in the pot and bring the water back to a rolling boil. Make sure that the jars are all upright and stable.

- Once the water starts boiling, cover the pot, and start timing,

- After following the recommended processing time, turn the heat off.

- Take the lid off and leave the jars in the pot for five minutes.

- Take the jars out of the pot and place them on a flat surface covered with a cloth kitchen towel.

- Leave the jars to cool down undisturbed for about 12 to 24 hours depending on what is stated in the recipe.

- After cooling, remove the rings and check the seals.

- Wipe the jars, label them with the date, and store them in your prepper pantry.

Preparing the ingredients would take varying amounts of time. For instance, raw packing ingredients wouldn't require much time compared to hot packing ingredients. This is why you need to familiarize yourself with the recipe so that you can plan your time wisely.

Make Sure There is Enough Headspace

Headspace refers to the gap between the contents of the jar and the rim. You need to measure the headspace carefully as some foods tend to expand when you process them in the water bath. Most recipes call for ¼ or ½-inch headspace. It's important to have enough headspace so that your food will be processed properly.

Take Note of Processing Times and Altitudes

The processing time is another important factor for you to take note of. Each recipe should state the exact processing time needed to preserve the ingredients. If you find a recipe that doesn't include a specific processing time, go online and search for a similar recipe. Don't worry though, the recipes here all have processing times for you to follow.

Generally, the processing times provided in recipes are for altitudes below 1,000 feet. It's important to know your altitude too as this could change the processing times of your food. Living in a place with a higher altitude means that you would have to process the food longer. If these altitudes are specified in the recipe, follow them to ensure the best and safest results.

Take Note of the Differences Between Raw and Hot Pack Preservation

Raw pack preservation involves adding raw ingredients into jars, then pouring a hot liquid into the jars before sealing them. Hot pack preservation involves adding the raw ingredients to the canning liquid, then allowing the ingredients to simmer for a certain amount of time before placing them into the jars.

If a recipe includes both preparation methods, make sure to follow the correct processing times when placing the jars in the canner.

Use New Lids Each Time You Process and Remove the Rings Before Storage

While it's possible to use canning jars over and over again for processing, you shouldn't do this for the lids. When it comes to canning, lids can only be used once. Then you can use them for other purposes, but not for canning. For the jars, if you will use them again, make sure to wash them thoroughly and sterilize them before processing.

Unlike lids, rings can be reused for canning purposes. Just wash them well first before using them again. Make sure to remove the rings before storing the jars as this is an important safety standard.

Make Sure That the Jars are Sealed Properly

After removing the rings, check the lids to make sure that the jars are sealed properly. The lids should be screwed onto the jars tightly. They shouldn't wobble when you take the rings off. If you notice any loose lids, check if the contents are still edible. If they are, consume them right away. Never store jars that have been improperly sealed.

Label and Store the Jars Properly

After making sure that the jars are properly sealed, label each of them with their processing date. This is important so that you can rotate your stocks regularly. Although foods that have been preserved through water bath canning can last for months or even years, you shouldn't wait for the expiration date to consume them.

Generally, foods canned at home last between 12 to 18 months. Over time, their quality declines in terms of texture, nutrition, and flavor. Although still safe to eat, they won't be as good as when you first processed them. For this reason, it's recommended that you schedule your canning sessions for every few months or so. That way, you can replace the old stocks with new ones and enjoy those old stocks before they get spoiled.

Make sure to store the preserved foods in a cool, dark place. If you already have a prepper pantry ready, store your jars there. If not, you can keep them in the basement, a cold storage area, or even in one of the cupboards in your pantry. The key here is to find a place where the temperature remains fairly constant to prevent early spoilage of your food items.

Wash All of Your Tools and Equipment After Use

Each time you finish a water bath canning session, you need to wash everything that you used. For best results, use hot, soapy water to clean your items, then rinse them well. After that, make sure to dry everything completely before storing them. Do this to maintain the quality of your water bath canning items so you can keep using them each time you need to preserve batches of food.

Never Make Up Your Own Canning Recipes

It can't be stated enough—follow canning recipes carefully. Remember that these recipes have been tested to ensure their safety. This is especially important if you are new to water bath canning. Avoid doing things like:

- Adding more vegetables to dilute relish or salsa recipes. Remember that vegetables are low-acid foods. Adding more than what is indicated in a recipe will mess up the balance and increase the risk of spoilage.

- Adding more starch to a recipe just to thicken it. Doing this reduces the ability of the heat to penetrate into the jars and the ingredients, thus resulting in under-processed or undercooked food.

These are just some examples of seemingly harmless recipe modifications that could result in unsafe results. Keep all of these tips in mind when it's time for you to start canning your first batch of preserves. The more you practice, the easier the process becomes. Then you will feel comfortable enough to try more complex recipes to add more variety to your stockpile.

Chapter 4:

Preparing Your Prepper Pantry

From the beginning of this book, you may have noticed the term "prepper pantry" being used quite often. This is because most people who become interested in preserving their own food at home want to start storing food for emergencies and other unexpected occurrences.

Simply put, a prepper pantry is a stockpile of various items that you store in one area or room in your home. Also known as a survival pantry, you can fill this space with preserved foods and other essential non-food items. The main purpose of having a prepper pantry is to provide what you and your family would need in case of an unexpected situation or emergency.

While you can store canned goods and other ready-made food items in your prepper pantry, making your own preserved foods is recommended if you want to have the most nutritious items in your storage space. Since you will be canning your own food at home, you won't have to worry about added chemicals or artificial ingredients that might compromise your health.

Before we dive into the different water bath canning recipes, let's focus on preparing your prepper pantry. That way, you can have it ready to store all of the delicious preserves you will process in your water bath canner.

The Benefits of Having a Prepper Pantry

You can build your prepper pantry either for short-term or long-term storage depending on your goals. If you want to have a prepper pantry for long-term food storage, adding canned foods is a good start. If you're wondering why having a prepper pantry is a good idea, here are some benefits to look forward to.

Food Security

When something bad happens like a natural disaster, a pandemic, or any other event that affects the general public, the first thing people do is flock to the local food shops to stock up on food supplies. In those situations, you would have to act quickly as all types of food will be flying off the shelves. If you have a prepper pantry at home that's filled with healthy and nutritious food, you won't have to join the other panic buyers. Instead, you can focus on keeping your family safe.

Peace of Mind

Even if nothing unexpected occurs, having a prepper pantry will give you peace of mind. Instead of worrying about potential catastrophes, you will feel confident that you can provide your family with the food they need while other people are fighting for whatever stocks are left in supermarkets. If you or any of your family members have allergies or other special dietary needs, having a prepper pantry becomes even more important as you won't have to worry about not finding the right foods to feed your family.

Convenience

This is another excellent benefit, especially if you live a very busy life. If some unexpected guests drop by your home, you will always have something to serve them. Simply take something from your stockpile, heat it up, and you're good to go! You can do the same thing if you don't have time to cook a proper meal for your family. Just make sure to replace the foods you have consumed with newly preserved foods to keep your survival pantry well-stocked.

Customization

Another great thing about having your own stockpile is that you can fill it with whatever foods you want. Just because you're preparing for emergency situations, that doesn't mean that you should settle for food that you don't like. When planning what to store in your survival pantry, make sure to include foods that you and your family like. Since you will be canning your own foods at home, you have the freedom to choose what to include and what to omit. That way, you can look forward to eating delicious foods even during emergencies or any other unexpected events.

Absolutely anyone can benefit from having a prepper pantry at home, and you don't have to break the bank to build one. Create a plan first, then start adding more foods to your stockpile over time. Before you know it, you will already have a fully stocked pantry along with all of these wonderful benefits to look forward to!

Tips for Planning Your Prepper Pantry

Having a prepper pantry at home is a truly wonderful thing, but building one isn't a simple task. You need to plan it well to ensure that the stockpile you create serves its purpose. To make things easier for you, here are some tips to keep in mind.

Create a Plan

As with any new endeavor, creating a plan for your prepper pantry is the first step. Think about your purpose or goal, what type of pantry you want to have, the foods you want to put in the pantry, and more. Take a moment to sit down and write (or type) all of your ideas. While brainstorming, you don't have to be too strict with yourself. After you have poured out all of your ideas on paper, go back to the list you have made. Pick out the best ideas you have and organize them. With a clear plan in front of you, building your prepper pantry will be a much easier task.

Determine the Location of Your Prepper Pantry

One of the most important things to decide when building a prepper pantry is where you will place it. Since you will be storing food in this space, you need a place that's predominantly dark and cool. It should also be free of pests and moisture. If you have a lot of rooms in your home, you can simply pick one to use as the location of your stockpile. If not, you can use an area of one of your rooms instead. Even though your prepper pantry won't be as big as you want it, if you find the right location, it will be a success.

Build Your Prepper Pantry Gradually

Once you have your plan and you have decided on the location, it's time to start putting your plan into action. For this, you don't have to go all out right away. Trying to fill your prepper pantry in a day will cost you a lot of money! It's better to start gradually. Go back to your plan, specifically the items (both food and non-food) that you want to store in your pantry. Add these items little by little so that you won't feel pressured. You want this to be a fun and fulfilling experience.

For instance, you can start with a few non-food items first since those aren't perishable. Then you can start planning which preserved foods to store. Since you will be preserving your own food through water bath canning, you have the freedom to choose which foods to process first. Keep going back to your plan. Each time you successfully add something to your pantry, cross it off your list. Continue doing this until you have stocked your prepper pantry with everything that you need.

Come Up With a Budget

Creating a budget for your stockpile will take some planning too. Right now, you may already have a food budget, which you use to feed yourself and your family every week or month. When working on your food budget, try to take a small portion from that, and use it to buy ingredients for your food preservation. Since you won't completely fill up your pantry with food immediately, you won't need a big budget for this purpose.

When it's time to shop for ingredients, try to search for discounts, sales, and other deals that will help you save money. You can even buy ingredients in bulk, then use these for food preservation and for your weekly meals. Take time to compare prices from different food shops and try to get your hands on coupons whenever possible. Doing all of these things may take some effort, but it will all be worth it once you see that your prepper pantry is filling up with essential items.

Focus on Nutrition and Variety

Think about these factors when deciding the foods to store in your prepper pantry. You want to avoid canned and frozen foods that are highly processed as they typically contain artificial ingredients that aren't good for your health. So when planning what foods to store in your stockpile, think about the nutrient content. That way, you will feel good about what you and your family will eat even in difficult situations.

To make things interesting, come up with different options too. When dealing with an emergency, having to eat the same thing each day might make you feel even more stressed. Fortunately, this doesn't have to be the case. You have the freedom to choose what goes into your pantry. Fill it with different types of food so you will have something to look forward to no matter how bleak the situation gets.

Rotate Your Stocks

Preserving your own food at home allows you to create delicious and nutritious food items with longer shelf lives. However, it's important to remember that home-canned foods don't last as long as processed, store-bought ones. This is because you won't be using chemicals or artificial additives in the preservation process.

This is why it's important to label each of your food jars with the processing date. Then you need to rotate your stocks regularly. This simply means that you regularly preserve new stocks through water bath canning, then replace the old ones with the new ones. When you will do this depends on the shelf life of your existing stocks. After replacing the old stocks with new ones, you can consume the old stocks. Include them in your weekly meal plan so that you can enjoy them without wasting any food.

Try to come up with a system for rotating your stocks. For instance, when planning what foods to preserve, group them according to their shelf life. That way, you can repeat the same process after a certain number of months for the purpose of rotation. Avoid replacing too many jars at the same time as you might end up with too much food that you need to consume. Finally, don't wait until the expiration date is too close as you might not be able to eat your old stocks before they get spoiled. If you can't eat all of your old stocks, consider gifting them to your friends and loved ones so they don't go to waste.

Start Meal Planning

Meal planning is a simple process that works very well with building a prepper pantry. This process typically involves planning your meals every week. It allows you to be aware of what you have and what you need. By meal planning, you can be more efficient at planning your budget and your stock-rotation system.

When it comes to planning your prepper pantry, the key is to go at your own pace. It can take a couple of weeks, a couple of months, or even a year or so to fully stock your pantry. As the days go by, keep checking your stocks and your list until you have completed everything you need. When you reach that point, all you have to do is to rotate your stocks regularly and enjoy the fruits of your efforts.

All About Meal Planning and How to Start

Meal planning is a very simple process. It involves setting a schedule to plan your meals for a certain period of time, usually one week. After planning your menu, write down all of the ingredients you need to cook the meals you have planned. When you have your list, you should go to the supermarket to buy everything you need. After that, you can prep the ingredients at home and cook all of your meals.

When you're done, allow the meals to cool down completely before covering the containers and storing them in your refrigerator. This will provide homemade meals for the whole week. All you need to do is reheat them when the time is right.

Meal planning is highly recommended when you're starting a new diet or when you just want to start eating healthier meals. It saves time and money, and it teaches you to make healthier food choices. By meal planning, you can also keep yourself updated on the stocks you have in your prepper pantry as you can include your old stocks in your meal plans. To start meal planning, here are some practical pointers:

- As with building your prepper pantry, start slow when planning meals. Start by planning one meal per week first (the one you usually skip because you're too busy to cook), then keep adding as the weeks go by.

- Before you start planning your meals for the week, check your refrigerator. If you have any leftover meals from the previous week, include them on the first day in the meal plan you are making. Just check those meals first to make sure that they aren't spoiled yet.

- When planning your menu, focus on easy, simple, nutrient-dense meals for you and your family.

- Check your prepper pantry regularly as well. If you see that you have any stocks that need to be rotated, make sure to include them in your meal plan for the week.

- After planning your menu, write down all of the ingredients you need. If you will also have a canning session for that week, include the ingredients you need for that as well.

- Before going to the supermarket, check the stocks you have in your kitchen or pantry. You might have leftover ingredients that you can use. In such a case, you may cross out any duplicate ingredients from your shopping list.

- Invest in high-quality food containers to store your meals in. Airtight containers that are microwave-safe are the best. Find containers of just the right size. It would also be better if you can stack the containers to make it easier to store them in your refrigerator.

- Add variety to your diet by trying different recipes. You can find tons of easy, tasty, and healthy recipes online. Compile all of the recipes that you and your family like so that you can keep going back to them.

Meal planning takes some getting used to, especially if you have never done it before. But if you consistently plan your meals every week, this process will soon become part of your routine. Then you will realize how efficient and enjoyable meal planning is!

Chapter 5:

Recipes for Canning Fruits

Now that you have learned the basics of water bath canning, it's time to put that knowledge to work. There are so many foods you can preserve through water bath canning. In this chapter, you will learn how to preserve different kinds of fruits.

Apricots

This is a lovely recipe for fresh apricots preserved in a light syrup. The syrup will preserve the natural flavors of the apricots as it won't make them too sweet.

Time: 50 minutes

Servings: 3-quart jars

Prep Time: 20 minutes

Processing Time: 30 minutes

Ingredients:

- 2 cups of sugar
- 6 cups of water
- 9 lbs apricots (rinsed, pits removed, cut in half)

Directions:

1. Prepare the jars by heating them up in the water bath canner. Heat up the water in the canner, but not to the point of boiling.
2. In a large pot, add the sugar and water.
3. Stir well until the sugar dissolves, then bring the mixture to a boil.

4. Place the apricot halves in the jars with the cut side facing down. Make sure that there is ½-inch of headspace.

5. Pour the syrup into the jars making sure that there is ½-inch of headspace.

6. Remove the air bubbles and add more syrup as needed.

7. Wipe the rims of the jars clean, then place the seal and ring.

8. Add the jars to the water bath canner, then bring the canner to a boil.

9. Once the water is boiling, cover the water bath canner and process for 30 minutes.

10. After processing, turn off the heat and take the lid off the canner.

11. Allow to rest for about 5 minutes before taking the jars out of the hot water.

12. Place the jars on a thick kitchen towel and allow them to cool down for up to 24 hours.

13. Remove the jars, check the seals, label, and store.

Blackberries

Blackberries are a type of short-season fruit. Preserving them means that you can eat this tasty berry all year round. Use fresh blackberries for flavorful and firm results.

Time: 30 minutes

Serving Size: 2-pint jars

Prep Time: 20 minutes

Processing Time: 10 minutes

Ingredients for the syrup:

- ¼ cup of water

- 2 cups of blackberries (fresh)

Ingredients for the blackberries:

- ½ tsp nutmeg (freshly grated)
- ½ cup of brandy
- 2 cups of sugar
- 2 cups of water
- 4 cups of blackberries
- 1 cinnamon stick

Directions:

1. Prepare the jars by heating them up in the water bath canner. Heat up the water in the canner, but not to the point of boiling.
2. In a saucepan, add the blackberries over medium heat.
3. Use a fork or a potato masher to mash the blackberries slightly.
4. Add the water, stir well, and bring the mixture to a simmer.
5. Allow to simmer for about 2 minutes.
6. Use a fine-mesh strainer to strain the blackberries over a bowl. Discard the fruit pulp or use it in another recipe.
7. In a pot, add the water, sugar, nutmeg, and cinnamon stick over medium heat. Stir everything together and bring the mixture to a boil.
8. Allow to boil for about 5 minutes.
9. Add the brandy, blackberries, and the strained blackberry juice. Stir everything together and bring the mixture to a boil while stirring constantly. Be careful when stirring so you don't damage the berries.
10. Use a slotted spoon to transfer the blackberries into the heated jars making sure that there is ½-inch of headspace.
11. Pour the blackberry syrup into the jars.
12. Remove the air bubbles and add more syrup as needed.

13. Wipe the rims of the jars clean, then place the seal and ring.

14. Add the jars to the water bath canner, then bring the canner to a boil.

15. Once the water is boiling, cover the water bath canner and process for 10 minutes.

16. After processing, turn off the heat and take the lid off the canner.

17. Allow to rest for about 5 minutes before taking the jars out of the hot water.

18. Place the jars on a thick kitchen towel and allow them to cool down for up to 24 hours.

19. Remove the jars, check the seals, label, and store.

Cherries

If you love adding cherries to baked goods and desserts, you should try canning your own cherries at home. Canning these fresh fruits in light syrup is the best way to do this.

Time: depends on the processing time

Servings: 4-quart jars

Prep Time: 20 minutes

Processing Time: depends on the altitude

Ingredients:

- 4 ½ cups of honey
- 12 cups of water

- 10 lbs of cherries

Directions:

1. Prepare the jars by heating them up in the water bath canner. Heat up the water in the canner, but not to the point of boiling.

2. In a saucepan, add the water and honey over medium heat.

3. Stir the ingredients together until the honey dissolves completely.

4. Pour ½ cup of syrup into each of the heated jars.

5. Add the cherries to each of the jars making sure that there is ½-inch of headspace.

6. Remove the air bubbles and add more syrup as needed.

7. Wipe the rims of the jars clean, then place the seal and ring.

8. Add the jars to the water bath canner, then bring the canner to a boil.

9. Once the water is boiling, cover the water bath canner and process based on your altitude:

    a) 25 minutes for altitudes between 0 and 1,000 ft

    b) 30 minutes for altitudes between 1,001 and 3,000 ft

    c) 35 minutes for altitudes between 3,001 and 6,000 ft

    d) 40 minutes for altitudes above 6,000 ft

10. After processing, turn off the heat and take the lid off the canner.

11. Allow to rest for about 5 minutes before taking the jars out of the hot water.

12. Place the jars on a thick kitchen towel and allow them to cool down for up to 24 hours.

13. Remove the jars, check the seals, label, and store.

Cranberries

Before canning whole cranberries, create a rich syrup to help preserve them. This is another seasonal fruit for you to preserve, especially if you're fond of cranberries.

Time: 35 minutes

Serving Size: 4-quart jars

Prep Time: 20 minutes

Processing Time: 15 minutes

Ingredients:

- ¾ cup of sugar
- 5 cups of water
- 12 lbs of cranberries (fresh, rinsed)

Directions:

1. Prepare the jars by heating them up in the water bath canner. Heat up the water in the canner, but not to the point of boiling.
2. In a pot, add the water and sugar over medium heat.
3. Stir the ingredients together and bring the mixture to a simmer.
4. When the mixture starts simmering, add the cranberries.
5. Allow to simmer for about 1 to 2 minutes until the berries are heated through and they are starting to crack.
6. Scoop the cranberries and the syrup into the heated canning jars making sure that there is ½-inch of headspace.
7. Remove the air bubbles and add more syrup as needed.
8. Wipe the rims of the jars clean, then place the seal and ring.
9. Add the jars to the water bath canner, then bring the canner to a boil.
10. Once the water is boiling, cover the water bath canner and process for 15 minutes.
11. After processing, turn off the heat and take the lid off the canner.
12. Allow to rest for about 5 minutes before taking the jars out of the hot water.

13. Place the jars on a thick kitchen towel and allow them to cool down for up to 24 hours.

14. Remove the jars, check the seals, label, and store.

Fruit Cocktail

If you like buying fruit cocktails in supermarkets, why don't you try making your own fruity mixture at home. Here is a basic recipe but you can always switch up the fruits.

Time: 50 minutes

Serving Size: 3-quart jars

Prep Time: 30 minutes

Processing Time: 20 minutes

Ingredients:

- 3 cups of sugar
- 4 cups of water
- 1 ½ lbs green grapes (seedless, slightly under ripe)
- 3 lbs peaches (fresh)
- 3 lbs pears (fresh)
- ⅔ lbs maraschino cherries (jarred)
- Lemon juice (for soaking the fruits)

Directions:

1. Rinse the grapes, then place them in a bowl filled with lemon juice.
2. Bring a pot of water to a boil over medium heat.
3. Once the water starts boiling, add the peaches and cook for about 1 to 2 minutes.
4. Transfer the peaches to a bowl filled with cold water, then slip the skins off.

5. Slice the peaches in half, remove the pits, and cut into cubes.

6. Add the peach cubes to the bowl with the grapes.

7. Peel the pears, cut them in half, and remove the cores.

8. Cut up the pears into cubes, then add them to the bowl.

9. Prepare the jars by heating them up in the water bath canner. Heat up the water in the canner, but not to the point of boiling.

10. In a pot, add the water and sugar over medium heat. Stir the ingredients together until the sugar dissolves completely. Bring to a boil.

11. Once the syrup starts boiling, turn the heat down. Allow to boil gently.

12. Drain and discard the lemon juice from the bowl with the mixed fruits.

13. Add ½ cup of boiling syrup into each of the heated jars.

14. Divide the cherries among the jars, then add the mixed fruits making sure that there is ½-inch of headspace.

15. Remove the air bubbles and add more syrup as needed.

16. Wipe the rims of the jars clean, then place the seal and ring.

17. Add the jars to the water bath canner, then bring the canner to a boil.

18. Once the water is boiling, cover the water bath canner and process for 20 minutes.

19. After processing, turn off the heat and take the lid off the canner.

20. Allow to rest for about 5 minutes before taking the jars out of the hot water.

21. Place the jars on a thick kitchen towel and allow them to cool down for up to 24 hours.

22. Remove the jars, check the seals, label, and store.

Grapes

Grapes that have been preserved through water bath canning maintain their texture and flavor. This is a wonderful thing to consider, especially if you're fond of grapes.

Time: depends on the processing time

Servings: 4-quart jars

Prep Time: 10 minutes

Processing Time: depends on the altitude

Ingredients:

- ¾ cups of sugar
- 5 cups of water
- 8 lbs of grapes (firm, slightly underripe)

Directions:

1. Wash the grapes and remove the stems.
2. Prepare the jars by heating them up in the water bath canner. Heat up the water in the canner, but not to the point of boiling.
3. Bring a pot of water to a boil over medium heat.
4. Once the water is boiling, add the grapes. Blanche the grapes for about 45 seconds to 1 minute.
5. Use a slotted spoon to remove the grapes and transfer them to a bowl.
6. In a saucepan, add the water and sugar over medium heat.
7. Stir the ingredients together until the sugar dissolves completely.
8. Add the grapes to the heated jars making sure that there is ½-inch of headspace.
9. Pour the hot syrup into each of the jars.
10. Remove the air bubbles and add more syrup as needed.
11. Wipe the rims of the jars clean, then place the seal and ring.
12. Add the jars to the water bath canner, then bring the canner to a boil.

13. Once the water is boiling, cover the water bath canner and process for 10 minutes. For varying altitudes, take note of the following processing times:

14. 20 minutes for altitudes between 0 and 1,000 feet

15. 25 minutes for altitudes between 1,001 and 3,000 feet

16. 30 minutes for altitudes between 3,001 and 6,000 feet

17. 35 minutes for altitudes above 6,001 feet

18. After processing, turn off the heat and take the lid off the canner.

19. Allow to rest for about 5 minutes before taking the jars out of the hot water.

20. Place the jars on a thick kitchen towel and allow them to cool down for up to 24 hours.

21. Remove the jars, check the seals, label, and store.

Kiwi

When choosing kiwis for canning, opt for firm fruits instead of mushy ones. As this fruit is processed, it will gain a lighter color and a milder flavor.

Time: 50 minutes

Serving Size: 4-quart jars

Prep Time: 30 minutes

Processing Time: 20 minutes

Ingredients:

- 2 cups of sugar
- 4 cups of water
- 12 lbs kiwi

Directions:

1. Wash the kiwi fruits, peel them, and slice as desired.
2. Prepare the jars by heating them up in the water bath canner. Heat up the water in the canner, but not to the point of boiling.
3. In a pot, add the water over medium heat and bring to a simmer.
4. Once the water starts to simmer, add the sugar. Mix well until the sugar dissolves completely. Bring to a gentle boil.
5. Add the kiwi slices to the pot. Mix gently and cook for about 2 to 3 minutes.
6. Fill the jars with the kiwi slices and syrup, making sure that there is ½-inch of headspace.
7. Remove the air bubbles and add more syrup as needed.
8. Wipe the rims of the jars clean, then place the seal and ring.
9. Add the jars to the water bath canner, then bring the canner to a boil.
10. Once the water is boiling, cover the water bath canner and process for 20 minutes.
11. After processing, turn off the heat and take the lid off the canner.
12. Allow to rest for about 5 minutes before taking the jars out of the hot water.
13. Place the jars on a thick kitchen towel and allow them to cool down for up to 24 hours.
14. Remove the jars, check the seals, label, and store.

Lemons

Although lemons are always available, it's still a good idea to can them at home. Having lemons in your prepper pantry allows you to use this fruit whenever you need it.

Time: 30 minutes

Serving Size: 3-quart jars

Prep Time: 25 minutes

Processing Time: 5 minutes

Ingredients:

- 6 cups of sugar
- 18 lemons (rinsed thoroughly)

Directions:

1. Prepare the jars by washing them thoroughly. Do the same for the lids and the rings. Sterilize everything well.
2. Use a sharp knife to slice each of the lemons into 6 slices.
3. Sprinkle sugar into one jar, then place 3 slices of lemon on top of it. Keep adding layers of sugar and lemon slices until you reach the top. The last layer should be a layer of sugar.
4. Cover the jar with a clean piece of cotton cloth, then secure the cloth using a rubber band.
5. Repeat the filling steps for the rest of the jars.
6. Place the jars in the refrigerator and leave them there overnight. By doing this, the sugar will melt and turn into syrup.
7. The next day, take the jars out. Leave them on the counter to warm up to room temperature.
8. Prepare the water bath canner by adding water to it and heating it up.
9. Open the jars and remove the cotton cloth. Wipe the rims of the jars clean, then place the seal and ring.
10. Add the jars to the water bath canner, then bring the canner to a boil.
11. Once the water is boiling, cover the water bath canner and process for 5 minutes.
12. After processing, turn off the heat and take the lid off the canner.
13. Allow to rest for about 5 minutes before taking the jars out of the hot water.
14. Place the jars on a thick kitchen towel and allow them to cool down for up to 24 hours.
15. Remove the jars, check the seals, label, and store.

Mango

You may can mangoes at home to preserve this fruit as it can get expensive when it's not in season. Mangoes are very versatile, which means you can use them in different ways.

Time: 40 minutes

Serving Size: 3-quart jars

Prep Time: 20 minutes

Processing Time: 20 minutes

Ingredients:

- ½ cup of sugar
- ¾ cup of lemon juice (fresh)
- 4 cups of water
- 18 mangoes

Directions:

1. Prepare the jars by heating them up in the water bath canner. Heat up the water in the canner, but not to the point of boiling.
2. Slice the mangoes, scoop the flesh out, and cut the flesh into cubes.
3. Fill the jars with the mango cubes making sure that there is ½-inch of headspace.
4. Pour ¼ cup of lemon juice into each of the jars. Set the jars aside while you prepare the syrup.
5. In a pot, add the water over medium heat.
6. Mix well until the sugar dissolves completely, then bring the mixture to a boil.
7. Pour the syrup into each of the jars with mango cubes.
8. Remove the air bubbles and add more syrup as needed.

9. Wipe the rims of the jars clean, then place the seal and ring.

10. Add the jars to the water bath canner, then bring the canner to a boil.

11. Once the water is boiling, cover the water bath canner and process for 20 minutes.

12. After processing, turn off the heat and take the lid off the canner.

13. Allow to rest for about 5 minutes before taking the jars out of the hot water.

14. Place the jars on a thick kitchen towel and allow them to cool down for up to 24 hours.

15. Remove the jars, check the seals, label, and store.

Peaches

Peaches are a versatile fruit that can be processed in a water bath canner easily. For this recipe, you will preserve the peaches in a light syrup to maintain their natural flavor.

Time: 1 hour, 20 minutes

Serving Size: 4-quart jars

Prep Time: 1 hour

Processing Time: 20 minutes

Ingredients:

- ⅛ cup of lemon juice
- ¾ cup of sugar
- 2 ¾ cups of water
- 9 lbs peaches
- Ice

Directions:

1. Prepare the jars by heating them up in the water bath canner. Heat up the water in the canner, but not to the point of boiling.

2. Fill a bowl with water and lemon juice.

3. Use a paring knife to cut the peaches in half, then remove the pits. Place the peach halves in the bowl of lemon water.

4. In a pot, add the water and sugar over medium heat. Stir well until the sugar dissolves, then bring the mixture to a boil.

5. Once the syrup is boiling, fill a bowl with water and ice.

6. Add the peach halves into the pot with the syrup and cook them for about 1 minute. If needed, cook the peach halves in batches.

7. Use a slotted spoon to transfer the peach halves to the bowl with ice water for about 1 minute.

8. Gently peel the skin off the peach halves, then place them in the heated jars with the cut side facing down.

9. Pour the syrup into each of the jars making sure that there is ½-inch of headspace.

10. Remove the air bubbles and add more syrup as needed.

11. Wipe the rims of the jars clean, then place the seal and ring.

12. Add the jars to the water bath canner, then bring the canner to a boil.

13. Once the water is boiling, cover the water bath canner and process for 20 minutes.

14. After processing, turn off the heat and take the lid off the canner.

15. Allow to rest for about 5 minutes before taking the jars out of the hot water.

16. Place the jars on a thick kitchen towel and allow them to cool down for up to 12 hours.

17. Remove the jars, check the seals, label, and store.

Pears

When choosing pears to can, opt for firm, ripe ones. Also, choose fruits that don't have spoiled spots to ensure that you only get the highest-quality fruits in your jars.

Time: 50 minutes

Serving Size: 4-quart jars

Prep Time: 20 minutes

Processing Time: 30 minutes

Ingredients:

- ½ cup of lemon juice (fresh)
- 6 cups of water (for preserving the pears)
- 16 cups of water (for treating the pears)
- 12 lbs pears (rinsed well)

Directions:

1. Prepare the jars by heating them up in the water bath canner. Heat up the water in the canner, but not to the point of boiling.
2. In a pot, add some water and bring to a boil.
3. In a bowl, add the water and lemon juice, then mix well.
4. Cut the pears in half or quarters. Remove the seeds and any spoiled spots.
5. Add the pear halves to the bowl. Soak them for about 2 to 3 minutes.
6. Place the pear halves in the heated jars.
7. Pour boiling water into each of the jars making sure that there is ½-inch of headspace.
8. Remove the air bubbles and add more water as needed.
9. Wipe the rims of the jars clean, then place the seal and ring.

10. Add the jars to the water bath canner, then bring the canner to a boil.

11. Once the water is boiling, cover the water bath canner and process for 30 minutes.

12. After processing, turn off the heat and take the lid off the canner.

13. Allow to rest for about 5 minutes before taking the jars out of the hot water.

14. Place the jars on a thick kitchen towel and allow them to cool down for up to 12 hours.

15. Remove the jars, check the seals, label, and store.

Plums

Plums are a very versatile fruit that can be used in different ways. For this recipe, you will be making spiced plums for a tasty and healthy canned treat.

Time: 40 minutes

Serving Size: 5-quart jars

Prep Time: 20 minutes

Processing Time: 20 minutes

Ingredients:

- 4 cups of honey
- 10 cups of water
- 8 lbs plums (rinsed well)
- 4 oranges (juiced, zested)
- 10 cinnamon sticks
- 30 cloves

Directions:

1. Prepare the jars by heating them up in the water bath canner. Heat up the water in the canner, but not to the point of boiling.
2. In a pot, add the water, cinnamon sticks, honey, and orange juice over medium heat. Stir the ingredients well and bring the mixture to a boil.
3. Once the mixture starts boiling, turn the heat down to low. Allow to simmer for about 10 minutes while stirring frequently.
4. While the syrup simmers, cut the plums in half and remove the pits.
5. Add the plum halves to the pot, then bring the mixture back to a boil while stirring frequently.
6. Once the mixture starts boiling, turn the heat off.
7. Prepare the jars by adding 1 teaspoon of orange zest and a few cloves to each of them.
8. Use a slotted spoon to fish out the cinnamon sticks, then add 2 sticks to each jar.
9. Add the plums and syrup into each of the jars making sure that there is ½-inch of headspace.
10. Remove the air bubbles and add more water as needed.
11. Wipe the rims of the jars clean, then place the seal and ring.
12. Add the jars to the water bath canner, then bring the canner to a boil.
13. Once the water is boiling, cover the water bath canner and process for 20 minutes.
14. After processing, turn off the heat and take the lid off the canner.
15. Allow to rest for about 5 minutes before taking the jars out of the hot water.
16. Place the jars on a thick kitchen towel and allow them to cool down for up to 24 hours.
17. Remove the jars, check the seals, label, and store.

Raspberries

It's very easy to preserve raspberries through water bath canning and the result is amazingly tasty. Eat the preserved fruits on their own or add them to various dishes.

Time: 25 minutes

Serving Size: 3-quart jars

Prep Time: 15 minutes

Processing Time: 10 minutes

Ingredients:

- 6 cups of sugar (granulated)
- 6 ¾ cups of water
- 9 lbs raspberries (fresh, rinsed well)

Directions:

1. Prepare the jars by heating them up in the water bath canner. Heat up the water in the canner, but not to the point of boiling.
2. In a pot, add the water and sugar over medium heat. Stir well until the sugar dissolves, then bring the mixture to a boil.
3. Once the mixture starts boiling, take the pot off the heat. Allow the syrup to cool down for about 5 minutes.
4. Add the raspberries into each of the jars making sure that there is ½-inch of headspace.
5. Pour the hot syrup into the jars.
6. Remove the air bubbles and add more syrup as needed.
7. Wipe the rims of the jars clean, then place the seal and ring.
8. Add the jars to the water bath canner, then bring the canner to a boil.
9. Once the water is boiling, cover the water bath canner and process for 10 minutes.
10. After processing, turn off the heat and take the lid off the canner.
11. Allow to rest for about 5 minutes before taking the jars out of the hot water.
12. Place the jars on a thick kitchen towel and allow them to cool down for up to 24 hours.

13. Remove the jars, check the seals, label, and store.

Chapter 6:

Recipes for Canning Vegetables

After canning different types of fruits, it's time to start canning veggies. The challenge with canning veggies is that most of them are low in acid. Because of this, you have to pickle some types of vegetables first before preserving them in your water bath canner. In this chapter, you will learn how to can different types of raw or pickled vegetables.

Candied Jalapeños

Candied jalapeños are wonderfully delicious with their hot and sweet flavors. Use these preserves as a versatile condiment in various dishes.

Time: 45 minutes

Serving Size: 3-quart jars

Prep Time: 20 minutes

Cook Time: 25 minutes

Ingredients:

- 1 tsp cinnamon
- 1 tsp ginger (fresh, grated)
- 1 tsp turmeric
- 1 ½ cups of white vinegar
- 3 cups of white sugar
- 3 lbs jalapeños (sliced)

Directions:

1. Prepare the jars by heating them up in the water bath canner. Heat up the water in the canner, but not to the point of boiling.
2. In a pot, add the sugar, vinegar, turmeric, cinnamon, and ginger over medium-high heat. Stir everything together and bring the mixture to a boil.
3. Once the mixture starts boiling, turn the heat down to low. Allow to simmer for about 5 to 7 minutes until it reduces into a syrup.
4. Turn the heat back up to medium-high and add the jalapeños to the pot.
5. Stir well and bring the mixture to a boil.
6. Once the mixture starts boiling, turn the heat down to low. Allow to simmer for about 5 minutes.
7. Add the jalapeños and syrup into each of the jars making sure that there is ½-inch of headspace.
8. Remove the air bubbles and add more syrup as needed.
9. Wipe the rims of the jars clean, then place the seal and ring.
10. Add the jars to the water bath canner, then bring the canner to a boil.
11. Once the water is boiling, cover the water bath canner and process for 10 minutes.
12. After processing, turn off the heat and take the lid off the canner.
13. Allow to rest for about 5 minutes before taking the jars out of the hot water.
14. Place the jars on a thick kitchen towel and allow them to cool down for up to 24 hours.
15. Remove the jars, check the seals, label, and store.

Dill Pickles

Here is an easy canning recipe for you to make your own dill pickles. The pickles you will preserve will be crunchy, tasty, and perfectly tangy.

Time: 45 minutes

Serving Size: 3-quart jars

Prep Time: 30 minutes

Cook Time: 15 minutes

Ingredients:

- ¼ tsp peppercorns (whole)
- ½ tsp mustard seeds
- 4 tbsp + 2 tsp salt
- ½ cup of cane sugar (preferably organic)
- 2 ½ cups + 1 tbsp water
- 2 ½ cups + 1 tbsp white vinegar
- 4 lbs pickling cucumbers (rinsed well)
- 1 bay leaf
- 2 allspice berries
- 2 cloves (whole)
- 6 sprigs of dill (fresh)

Directions:

1. Prepare the jars by heating them up in the water bath canner. Heat up the water in the canner, but not to the point of boiling.

2. In a saucepan, add the vinegar, water, salt, and sugar over medium heat.

3. Add the mustard seeds, peppercorns, bay leaf, cloves, and allspice berries to a cheesecloth, then wrap them up to make a spice bag.

4. Add the spice bag to the saucepan. Stir everything together, then bring the mixture to a boil.

5. Once the mixture starts boiling, turn the heat down to low. Allow to simmer for about 15 minutes while stirring occasionally.

6. Slice the cucumbers and add them into each of the jars making sure that there is ½-inch of headspace.

7. Add 2 sprigs of dill into each of the jars too.

8. Pour the hot brine into the jars.

9. Remove the air bubbles and add more brine as needed.

10. Wipe the rims of the jars clean, then place the seal and ring.

11. Add the jars to the water bath canner, then bring the canner to a boil.

12. Once the water is boiling, cover the water bath canner and process for 15 minutes.

13. After processing, turn off the heat and take the lid off the canner.

14. Allow to rest for about 5 minutes before taking the jars out of the hot water.

15. Place the jars on a thick kitchen towel and allow them to cool down for up to 24 hours.

16. Remove the jars, check the seals, label, and store.

Mushrooms

For this recipe, you will marinate the mushrooms first before preserving them. This helps with the preservation process so that you can use the water bath canning method.

Time: 40 minutes

Serving Size: 4-quart jars

Prep Time: 20 minutes

Cook Time: 20 minutes

Ingredients:

- 1 tbsp basil (dried)

- 1 tbsp oregano (dried)
- 1 tbsp pickling salt
- ¼ cup of pimento (diced)
- ½ cup of lemon juice (bottled)
- ½ cup of onions (finely chopped)
- 2 cups of olive oil
- 3 cups of white vinegar (preferably with 5% acidity)
- 7 lbs mushrooms (whole, rinsed well, half of the stems cut off)
- 2 cloves of garlic (cut in quarters)
- 25 black peppercorns (whole)
- Water (for cooking the mushrooms)

Directions:

1. In a pot, add the water, lemon juice, and mushrooms over medium heat. Stir everything well, then bring the mixture to a boil.
2. Once the mixture starts boiling, turn the heat down to low. Cover the pot with a lid and allow to simmer for about 5 minutes.
3. Drain and discard the liquid from the pot. Cover the pot and set aside.
4. Prepare the jars by heating them up in the water bath canner. Heat up the water in the canner, but not to the point of boiling.
5. In another pot, add the vinegar, olive oil, basil, oregano, salt, pimiento, and onion over medium heat. Stir everything well, then bring the mixture to a boil.
6. Once the mixture starts boiling, take the pot off the heat.
7. Divide the garlic and peppercorns between the jars.
8. Fill each of the jars with mushrooms making sure that there is ½-inch of headspace.

9. Pour the marinade into the jars and mix well.

10. Remove the air bubbles and add more marinade as needed.

11. Wipe the rims of the jars clean, then place the seal and ring.

12. Add the jars to the water bath canner, then bring the canner to a boil.

13. Once the water is boiling, cover the water bath canner and process for 20 minutes.

14. After processing, turn off the heat and take the lid off the canner.

15. Allow to rest for about 5 minutes before taking the jars out of the hot water.

16. Place the jars on a thick kitchen towel and allow them to cool down for up to 24 hours.

17. Remove the jars, check the seals, label, and store.

Pickled Asparagus

You need to pickle asparagus first before preserving it through water bath canning. After pickling, this becomes a shelf-stable veggie that deserves a place in your prepper pantry.

Time: 25 minutes

Serving Size: 3-quart jars

Prep Time: 15 minutes

Cook Time: 10 minutes

Ingredients for the asparagus:

- 10 ½ lbs asparagus spears (fresh, ends trimmed)
- A handful of dill weed (fresh)

Ingredients for the pickling brine:

- 3 tsp allspice berries
- 6 tsp mustard seeds

- 6 tsp coriander seeds

- 3 tbsp dill seeds

- 6 tbsp cane sugar

- ¾ cup of pickling salt

- 7 ½ cups of water

- 7 ½ cups of white vinegar (preferably with 5% acidity)

- 12 cloves of garlic (minced)

Directions:

1. Prepare the jars by heating them up in the water bath canner. Heat up the water in the canner, but not to the point of boiling.

2. Trim the ends of the asparagus spears to match the height of your canning jars making sure that there is ¼-inch headspace from the top.

3. Pack the asparagus spears into each of the heated canning jars. Also, add some sprigs of fresh dill weed between the asparagus spears.

4. In a saucepan, add all of the brine ingredients over medium heat. Stir everything together and bring the mixture to a boil.

5. Keep boiling for about 3 minutes.

6. Pour the brine into each of the jars making sure to include the solid components as well.

7. Remove the air bubbles and add more brine as needed.

8. Wipe the rims of the jars clean, then place the seal and ring.

9. Add the jars to the water bath canner, then bring the canner to a boil.

10. Once the water is boiling, cover the water bath canner and process for 10 minutes.

11. After processing, turn off the heat and take the lid off the canner.

12. Allow to rest for about 5 minutes before taking the jars out of the hot water.

13. Place the jars on a thick kitchen towel and allow them to cool down for up to 24 hours.

14. Remove the jars, check the seals, label, and store.

Pickled Beets

Here is an old-fashioned recipe for you to pickle beets, then preserve them through water bath canning. If you love beets, you'll surely enjoy the results.

Time: 55 minutes

Serving Size: 4-quart jars

Prep Time: 30 minutes

Cook Time: 25 minutes

Ingredients:

- 4 tsp canning salt
- 6 cups of granulated sugar
- 6 cups of white vinegar
- 10 lbs beets (rinsed well, leaves removed)
- Water (for cooking the beets)

Directions:

1. In a pot, add the water and the beets over medium heat, then bring to a boil.
2. Once the mixture starts boiling, cook the beets for about 15 minutes or until fork-tender. The actual cooking time will depend on the size of the beets
3. When the beets are tender enough, transfer them to a bowl with cold water to stop the cooking process.
4. Once the beets have cooled down, peel off the skins, and slice them thinly.
5. Prepare the jars by heating them up in the water bath canner. Heat up the water in the canner, but not to the point of boiling.

6. In another pot, add the vinegar and sugar over medium heat. Stir until the sugar dissolves, then bring the mixture to a boil.

7. Once the mixture starts boiling, take the pot off the heat.

8. Fill each of the jars with 1 teaspoon of canning salt and the sliced beets making sure that there is ½-inch of headspace.

9. Pour the brine into the jars and mix well.

10. Remove the air bubbles and add more brine as needed.

11. Wipe the rims of the jars clean, then place the seal and ring.

12. Add the jars to the water bath canner, then bring the canner to a boil.

13. Once the water is boiling, cover the water bath canner and process for 10 minutes.

14. After processing, turn off the heat and take the lid off the canner.

15. Allow to rest for about 5 minutes before taking the jars out of the hot water.

16. Place the jars on a thick kitchen towel and allow them to cool down for up to 24 hours.

17. Remove the jars, check the seals, label, and store.

Pickled Carrots

Pickling carrots is an easy task. You can either grow your own carrots or buy them from the supermarket, then preserve them by following this delicious recipe.

Time: 40 minutes

Serving Size: 3-quart jars

Prep Time: 20 minutes

Cook Time: 20 minutes

Ingredients for the brine:

- ½ cup of pickling salt
- 4 cups of water

- 4 cups of white vinegar

Ingredients for the carrots:

- 1 tbsp dill seed
- 6 lbs baby carrots (scrubbed)
- 6 cloves of garlic (peeled, sliced in half lengthwise)
- 6 heads of flowering dill (fresh)

Directions:

1. Prepare the jars by heating them up in the water bath canner. Heat up the water in the canner, but not to the point of boiling.
2. In a pot, add all of the brine ingredients over medium heat. Stir until the salt dissolves, then bring the mixture to a boil.
3. Once the mixture starts boiling, take the pot off the heat.
4. Fill each of the jars with garlic, dill, and baby carrots making sure that there is ½-inch of headspace.
5. Sprinkle dill seeds into each of the jars.
6. Pour the brine into the jars.
7. Remove the air bubbles and add more brine as needed.
8. Wipe the rims of the jars clean, then place the seal and ring.
9. Add the jars to the water bath canner, then bring the canner to a boil.
10. Once the water is boiling, cover the water bath canner and process for 20 minutes for altitudes up to 2,999 feet. Process for 20 minutes for altitudes above 3,000 feet.
11. After processing, turn off the heat and take the lid off the canner.
12. Allow to rest for about 5 minutes before taking the jars out of the hot water.
13. Place the jars on a thick kitchen towel and allow them to cool down for up to 24 hours.
14. Remove the jars, check the seals, label, and store.

Pickled Eggplants

Have you ever tried pickled eggplants before? This preserved veggie pairs perfectly with meat, olives, cheese, and other finger foods. They go well with sandwiches too.

Time: depends on the altitude

Serving Size: 3-quart jars

Prep Time: 20 minutes

Cook Time: depends on the altitude

Ingredients:

- ⅓ cup of kosher salt
- 3 ½ cups of water
- 3 ½ cups of white vinegar
- 5 lbs eggplants (stems removed, sliced or cut into cubes)
- 6 bay leaves
- 6 cloves of garlic (minced)
- 6 heads of dill (chopped)

Directions:

1. Prepare the jars by heating them up in the water bath canner. Heat up the water in the canner, but not to the point of boiling.
2. In a pot, add the water and vinegar over medium heat, then bring to a boil.
3. Once the mixture starts boiling, take the pot off the heat.
4. Divide the garlic cloves, dill heads, and bay leaves among the jars.
5. Fill each of the jars with the eggplant slices too.
6. Pour the brine into the jars making sure that there is ¼-inch of headspace.

7. Remove the air bubbles and add more brine as needed.

8. Wipe the rims of the jars clean, then place the seal and ring.

9. Add the jars to the water bath canner, then bring the canner to a boil.

10. Once the water is boiling, cover the water bath canner and process for 15 minutes for altitudes below 1,000 feet. For varying altitudes, take note of the following processing times:

    a) 20 minutes for altitudes between 1,001 and 3,000 feet

    b) 25 minutes for altitudes between 3,001 and 6,000 feet

    c) 30 minutes for altitudes above 6,001 feet

11. After processing, turn off the heat and take the lid off the canner.

12. Allow to rest for about 5 minutes before taking the jars out of the hot water.

13. Place the jars on a thick kitchen towel and allow them to cool down for up to 12 hours.

14. Remove the jars, check the seals, label, and store.

Pickled Green Beans

These pickled green beans are wonderfully crunchy and flavorful. They deserve a place in your prepper pantry because they are very versatile as well.

Time: 50 minutes

Serving Size: 4-quart jars

Prep Time: 10 minutes

Cook Time: 40 minutes

Ingredients:

- 2 tsp cayenne pepper
- ½ cup of salt

- 5 cups of water

- 5 cups of white vinegar

- 4 lbs green beans (fresh)

- 8 cloves of garlic

- 8 sprigs of dill (fresh)

Directions:

1. Prepare the jars by heating them up in the water bath canner. Heat up the water in the canner, but not to the point of boiling.

2. Trim the green beans so that they can fit into your canning jars.

3. In a pot, add the water, salt, and white vinegar over medium heat. Stir well and bring the mixture to a boil.

4. Once the mixture starts to boil, prepare the jars.

5. In each jar, add 2 cloves of garlic, 2 sprigs of fresh dill, and ½ teaspoon of cayenne pepper.

6. Fill each of the jars with the green beans making sure that there is ½-inch of headspace.

7. Pour the brine into the jars.

8. Remove the air bubbles and add more brine as needed.

9. Wipe the rims of the jars clean, then place the seal and ring.

10. Add the jars to the water bath canner, then bring the canner to a boil.

11. Once the water is boiling, cover the water bath canner and process for 40 minutes.

12. After processing, turn off the heat and take the lid off the canner.

13. Allow to rest for about 5 minutes before taking the jars out of the hot water.

14. Place the jars on a thick kitchen towel and allow them to cool down for up to 24 hours.

15. Remove the jars, check the seals, label, and store.

Pickled Mixed Veggies

If you liked the recipe for fruit cocktail, you might enjoy this recipe too. Here, you will mix different veggies and pickle them in a garlicky brine.

Time: 40 minutes

Serving Size: 3-quart jars

Prep Time: 30 minutes

Cook Time: 10 minutes

Ingredients:

- 1 ½ tsp red pepper flakes
- 1 tbsp kosher salt
- 1 cup of sugar
- 3 cups of water
- 3 cups of white vinegar
- ¾ lb green beans (trimmed)
- **1 ⅓ lbs cauliflower florets**
- 2 ears of corn (husks removed, rinsed well, sliced)
- 2 onions (sliced into wedges)
- 3 red sweet peppers (seeded, sliced)
- 3 carrots (peeled, sliced)
- 18 cloves of garlic (smashed)
- Water (for cooking the vegetables)

Directions:

1. In a pot, add water with the cauliflower, corn, green beans, carrots, onions, and peppers over medium heat. Stir well and bring the mixture to a boil.

2. Once the mixture starts to boil, cook for about 3 minutes.

3. Drain and discard the water.

4. Prepare the jars by heating them up in the water bath canner. Heat up the water in the canner, but not to the point of boiling.

5. In another pot, add the water, sugar, salt, and vinegar over medium heat. Stir well until the sugar and salt dissolve, then bring the mixture to a boil.

6. In each jar, add 6 cloves of garlic, ½ teaspoon of red pepper flakes, and the cooked vegetables making sure that there is ½-inch of headspace.

7. Pour the brine into the jars.

8. Remove the air bubbles and add more brine as needed.

9. Wipe the rims of the jars clean, then place the seal and ring.

10. Add the jars to the water bath canner, then bring the canner to a boil.

11. Once the water is boiling, cover the water bath canner and process for 10 minutes.

12. After processing, turn off the heat and take the lid off the canner.

13. Allow to rest for about 5 minutes before taking the jars out of the hot water.

14. Place the jars on a thick kitchen towel and allow them to cool down for up to 24 hours.

15. Remove the jars, check the seals, label, and store.

Pickled Onions

If you grow your own onions and you have a bountiful harvest, pickling them is a great option. This allows you to preserve your harvest and store it in your prepper pantry.

Time: 30 minutes

Serving Size: 4-quart jars

Prep Time: 20 minutes

Cook Time: 10 minutes

Ingredients:

- 2 cups of apple cider vinegar
- 2 cups of white vinegar
- 3 lbs onions (rinsed well)
- 1 clove of garlic (peeled, crushed)

Directions:

1. Prepare the jars by heating them up in the water bath canner. Heat up the water in the canner, but not to the point of boiling.
2. Peel the onions, then rinse them again.
3. Slice the onions into rings or wedges.
4. In a pot, add the garlic clove, apple cider vinegar, and white vinegar over medium heat. Stir well, then bring the mixture to a boil.
5. Once the mixture starts to boil, turn the heat down to low. Allow to simmer for about 5 minutes.
6. Add the onion slices to the jars making sure that there is ½-inch of headspace.
7. Pour the vinegar mixture into the jars.
8. Remove the air bubbles and add more vinegar as needed.
9. Wipe the rims of the jars clean, then place the seal and ring.
10. Add the jars to the water bath canner, then bring the canner to a boil.
11. Once the water is boiling, cover the water bath canner and process for 10 minutes.
12. After processing, turn off the heat and take the lid off the canner.

13. Allow to rest for about 5 minutes before taking the jars out of the hot water.

14. Place the jars on a thick kitchen towel and allow them to cool down for up to 24 hours.

15. Remove the jars, check the seals, label, and store.

Spicy Pickled Garlic

To process low-acid veggies in a water bath canner safely, you need to pickle them first. Here is a recipe for you to do this with garlic.

Time: depends on the processing time

Serving Size: 3-quart jars

Prep Time: 20 minutes

Cook Time: depends on the processing time

Ingredients:

- ¾ tsp red pepper flakes
- ¾ tsp thyme (dried)
- 1 ½ tsp canning salt
- 3 tsp chili powder
- 3 ½ lbs garlic cloves (peeled)
- 6 cups of white vinegar (preferably with 5% acidity)
- 1 ½ cup of cane sugar

Directions:

1. Prepare the jars by heating them up in the water bath canner. Heat up the water in the canner, but not to the point of boiling.

2. In a saucepan, add the vinegar, water, salt, thyme, chili powder, and red pepper flakes over medium-high heat.

3. Stir everything together, then bring the mixture to a boil. Allow to boil while you prepare the jars.

4. Add the garlic cloves into each of the jars making sure that there is ½-inch of headspace.

5. Pour the hot brine into the jars.

6. Remove the air bubbles and add more brine as needed.

7. Wipe the rims of the jars clean, then place the seal and ring.

8. Add the jars to the water bath canner, then bring the canner to a boil.

9. Once the water is boiling, cover the water bath canner and process for 10 minutes for altitudes of 1,000 feet and below. For varying altitudes, take note of the following processing times:

    a) 15 minutes for altitudes between 1,001 and 6,000 feet

    b) 20 minutes for altitudes above 6,001 feet

10. After processing, turn off the heat and take the lid off the canner.

11. Allow to rest for about 5 minutes before taking the jars out of the hot water.

12. Place the jars on a thick kitchen towel and allow them to cool down for up to 24 hours.

13. Remove the jars, check the seals, label, and store.

Tomatoes

Canning whole tomatoes is a good idea if you like using tomatoes when cooking. That way, you can still enjoy tomatoes even during the winter months.

Time: 1 hour, 40 minutes

Serving Size: 4-quart jars

Prep Time: 15 minutes

Cook Time: 1 hour, 25 minutes

Ingredients:

- 8 tbsp lemon juice (concentrated)
- 13 lbs tomatoes (preferably Roma tomatoes, rinsed well)
- Water (for blanching the tomatoes)
- Water (cold, for blanching the tomatoes)

Directions:

1. Use a sharp knife to score the tomatoes.
2. In a pot, add water, and bring to a boil over medium heat.
3. Once the water starts boiling, add the tomatoes. Blanche them for about 1 minute.
4. Use a slotted spoon to take out the tomatoes, and transfer them to a bowl filled with cold water.
5. Prepare the jars by heating them up in the water bath canner. Heat up the water in the canner, but not to the point of boiling.
6. When the tomatoes are cool enough to handle, peel the skins off the tomatoes.
7. Add the peeled tomatoes (and their juices) to a bowl.
8. Add 2 tablespoons of concentrated lemon juice into each of the jars.
9. Fill the jars with the tomatoes and the tomato liquid making sure that there is ½-inch of headspace.
10. Remove the air bubbles and add water as needed.
11. Wipe the rims of the jars clean, then place the seal and ring.
12. Add the jars to the water bath canner, then bring the canner to a boil.
13. Once the water is boiling, cover the water bath canner and process for 1 hour and 25 minutes.
14. After processing, turn off the heat and take the lid off the canner.
15. Allow to rest for about 5 minutes before taking the jars out of the hot water.

16. Place the jars on a thick kitchen towel and allow them to cool down for up to 24 hours.

17. Remove the jars, check the seals, label, and store.

Chapter 7:

Recipes for Canning Jams and Jellies

Jams and jellies are the best types of food to preserve through water bath canning, and there are so many options for you to choose from! This chapter features easy jam and jelly recipes you can start with as you learn how to master the process of water bath canning.

3-Berry Jam

This lovely recipe combines different types of berries. That way, you can enjoy the taste of these berries all year long!

Time: 20 minutes

Serving Size: 4-pint jars

Prep Time: 10 minutes

Processing Time: 10 minutes

Ingredients:

- 4 tbsp pectin (powdered)
- ¼ cup of lemon juice (bottled)
- 3 cups of blackberries
- 3 cups of blueberries
- 3 cups of raspberries
- 10 cups of sugar (granulated)

Directions:

1. Prepare the jars by heating them up in the water bath canner. Heat up the water in the canner, but not to the point of boiling.

2. In a pot, add the blackberries, blueberries, raspberries, and lemon juice over medium heat.

3. Stir everything together and use a potato masher to mash the berries slightly.

4. Add the pectin powder and mix well.

5. Bring the berry mixture to a rolling boil while stirring constantly.

6. Once the mixture starts boiling, add the sugar.

7. Mix well and return the mixture to a boil. Continue boiling for about 1 minute while stirring constantly.

8. Take the pot off the heat and use a spoon to remove any foam on the top.

9. Use a ladle and a funnel to spoon the jam into the jars making sure that there is ¼-inch of headspace.

10. Remove the air bubbles and add more jam as needed.

11. Wipe the rims of the jars clean, then place the seal and ring.

12. Add the jars to the water bath canner, then bring the canner to a boil.

13. Once the water is boiling, cover the water bath canner and process for 10 minutes.

14. After processing, turn off the heat and take the lid off the canner.

15. Allow to rest for about 5 minutes before taking the jars out of the hot water.

16. Place the jars on a thick kitchen towel and allow them to cool down for up to 24 hours.

17. Remove the jars, check the seals, label, and store.

Coconut and Pineapple Jam

This tasty and refreshing jam is very easy to make. The wonderful combination of ingredients will keep you wanting more.

Time: 30 minutes

Serving Size: 4-pint jars

Prep Time: 20 minutes

Processing Time: 10 minutes

Ingredients:

- 6 tbsp fruit pectin
- ½ cup of coconut (shredded, sweetened)
- ⅔ cup of coconut water (you can also use coconut rum)
- 4 ⅔ cups of pineapple (crushed)
- 6 ⅔ cups of white sugar (granulated)

Directions:

1. Prepare the jars by heating them up in the water bath canner. Heat up the water in the canner, but not to the point of boiling.
2. In a pot, add the pineapples over medium heat.
3. Use a potato masher to mash the pineapples slightly, then bring to a boil.
4. Add the pectin powder and mix well.
5. Bring the mixture to a boil while stirring constantly.
6. Once the mixture starts boiling, add the sugar, coconut, and coconut water.
7. Mix well until the sugar dissolves completely, then return the mixture to a boil while stirring constantly.
8. Turn the heat down while you fill the jars.
9. Use a ladle and a funnel to spoon the jam into the jars making sure that there is ¼-inch of headspace.
10. Remove the air bubbles and add more jam as needed.

11. Wipe the rims of the jars clean, then place the seal and ring.

12. Add the jars to the water bath canner, then bring the canner to a boil.

13. Once the water is boiling, cover the water bath canner and process for 10 minutes.

14. After processing, turn off the heat and take the lid off the canner.

15. Allow to rest for about 5 minutes before taking the jars out of the hot water.

16. Place the jars on a thick kitchen towel and allow them to cool down for up to 24 hours.

17. Remove the jars, check the seals, label, and store.

Orange and Fig Jam

Combining the fresh figs with citrus flavors creates a delicious jam that you can use on desserts, bread, and more. This jam is easy to make and you don't need pectin for it.

Time: 50 minutes (sitting time not included)

Serving Size: 5-pint jars

Prep Time: 40 minutes

Processing Time: 10 minutes

Ingredients:

- 1 tbsp lemon zest
- 3 tbsp orange zest
- ½ cup of Grand Marnier
- 2 cups of sugar
- 4 ½ cups of figs (fresh, stems removed, sliced into ½-inch pieces)
- A pinch of salt

Directions:

1. In a pot, add the lemon zest, orange zest, figs, salt, and Grand Marnier.
2. Mix all of the ingredients together well.
3. Allow to sit for about 1 hour while stirring occasionally.
4. After 1 hour, place the pot over medium heat.
5. Add the sugar, mix well until the sugar dissolves completely, then bring the mixture to a boil.
6. Turn the heat down to low and allow to boil for about 30 minutes. Use a potato masher to mash the figs.
7. After about 15 minutes, prepare the jars by heating them up in the water bath canner. Heat up the water in the canner, but not to the point of boiling.
8. After boiling the jam, take the pot off the heat.
9. Use a ladle and a funnel to spoon the jam into the jars making sure that there is ¼-inch of headspace.
10. Remove the air bubbles and add more jam as needed.
11. Wipe the rims of the jars clean, then place the seal and ring.
12. Add the jars to the water bath canner, then bring the canner to a boil.
13. Once the water is boiling, cover the water bath canner and process for 10 minutes.
14. After processing, turn off the heat and take the lid off the canner.
15. Allow to rest for about 5 minutes before taking the jars out of the hot water.
16. Place the jars on a thick kitchen towel and allow them to cool down for up to 24 hours.
17. Remove the jars, check the seals, label, and store.

Salted Cantaloupe Jam

A lot of people wouldn't even think of making jam out of cantaloupes. But one taste of this mouthwatering jam and it might be one of your favorites!

Time: 40 minutes

Serving Size: 4-pint jars

Prep Time: 30 minutes

Processing Time: 10 minutes

Ingredients:

- 1 tsp vanilla extract
- 1 ½ tsp salt
- 2 tbsp lemon juice (freshly squeezed)
- 5 tbsp pectin (powdered)
- 4 cups of sugar (granulated, divided)
- 6 cups of cantaloupe (very ripe, peeled, diced)

Directions:

1. Prepare the jars by heating them up in the water bath canner. Heat up the water in the canner, but not to the point of boiling.
2. In a pot, add the lemon juice, cantaloupe, and 3 ½ cups of sugar over medium heat.
3. Stir all of the ingredients together and bring the mixture to a rolling boil.
4. Once the mixture starts boiling, add the pectin and the rest of the sugar. Whisk until well combined, then bring back to a rolling boil.
5. Allow to boil for about 2 to 3 minutes until it thickens to the right consistency.
6. Take the pot off the heat.
7. Add the salt and vanilla extract, then mix well.
8. Use a ladle and a funnel to spoon the jam into the jars making sure that there is ½-inch of headspace.
9. Remove the air bubbles and add more jam as needed.

10. Wipe the rims of the jars clean, then place the seal and ring.

11. Add the jars to the water bath canner, then bring the canner to a boil.

12. Once the water is boiling, cover the water bath canner and process for 10 minutes.

13. After processing, turn off the heat and take the lid off the canner.

14. Allow to rest for about 5 minutes before taking the jars out of the hot water.

15. Place the jars on a thick kitchen towel and allow them to cool down for up to 24 hours.

16. Remove the jars, check the seals, label, and store.

Zucchini Jam

This zucchini jam has subtle ginger and lemon flavors making it the perfect spread with warm pastries like scones. Make sure to use fresh zucchinis for this recipe!

Time: 1 hour

Serving Size: 4-pint jars

Prep Time: 50 minutes

Processing Time: 10 minutes

Ingredients:

- 4 cups of sugar
- 2 cups of water
- 4 cups of zucchini (shredded)
- 1 4-inch piece of ginger (fresh, peeled, minced)
- 4 lemons

Directions:

1. Use a grater to zest the lemons.

2. Cut the lemons in half and squeeze the juices out.

3. Remove the seeds from the juice and set aside.

4. Chop the white pith of the lemons roughly.

5. In a pot, add the lemon seeds, chopped pith, and water over medium heat. Stir the ingredients together and bring the mixture to a boil.

6. Once the mixture starts to boil, turn the heat down to low. Allow to simmer for about 30 minutes until you get about ½ cup of thick gel.

7. Use a slotted spoon to remove the seeds and pith from the pot.

8. Prepare the jars by heating them up in the water bath canner. Heat up the water in the canner, but not to the point of boiling.

9. In the pot with the thick gel, add the lemon juice, lemon zest, zucchini, ginger, and sugar.

10. Stir all of the ingredients together and bring the mixture to a rolling boil.

11. Allow to boil for about 10 minutes until you are satisfied with the consistency.

12. Use a ladle and a funnel to spoon the jam into the jars making sure that there is ¼-inch of headspace.

13. Remove the air bubbles and add more jam as needed.

14. Wipe the rims of the jars clean, then place the seal and ring.

15. Add the jars to the water bath canner, then bring the canner to a boil.

16. Once the water is boiling, cover the water bath canner and process for 10 minutes.

17. After processing, turn off the heat and take the lid off the canner.

18. Allow to rest for about 5 minutes before taking the jars out of the hot water.

19. Place the jars on a thick kitchen towel and allow them to cool down for up to 24 hours.

20. Remove the jars, check the seals, label, and store.

Corn Cob Jelly

If you have a lot of leftover corn cobs, make some jelly out of them. Here is a recipe for a sweet, spreadable jelly with a wonderful flavor.

Time: depends on the altitude

Serving Size: 4-pint jars

Prep Time: 50 minutes

Cook Time: depends on the altitude

Ingredients:

- ½ cup of fruit pectin
- 6 cups of sugar
- 16 cups of water
- 24 corn cobs (fresh, chopped into 4-inch pieces)

Directions:

1. In a saucepan, add the water and corn cobs over medium heat. Stir the ingredients together and bring the mixture to a boil.
2. Once the mixture starts boiling, turn the heat down to low. Simmer for about 35 to 40 minutes.
3. Place a fine-mesh sieve on top of a bowl, then cover it with 2 sheets of cheesecloth.
4. Pour the corn cob mixture into the sieve. Allow the liquid to drip into the bowl naturally without squeezing or pressing.
5. Prepare the jars by heating them up in the water bath canner. Heat up the water in the canner, but not to the point of boiling.
6. Pour the corn cob juice into a pot over medium heat.
7. Add the pectin powder and mix well.

8. Bring the mixture to a boil while stirring constantly. Allow to boil for about 1 minute.

9. Add the sugar and mix well until the sugar dissolves completely. Return the mixture to a boil. Allow to boil for about 5 minutes.

10. Take the pot off the heat and use a spoon to remove any foam on the top.

11. Use a ladle to pour the jelly into the jars making sure that there is ¼-inch of headspace.

12. Remove the air bubbles and add more jelly as needed.

13. Wipe the rims of the jars clean, then place the seal and ring.

14. Add the jars to the water bath canner, then bring the canner to a boil.

15. Once the water is boiling, cover the water bath canner and process for 5 minutes for altitudes of 1,000 feet and below. For varying altitudes, take note of the following processing times:

    a) 10 minutes for altitudes between 1,001 and 6,000 feet

    b) 15 minutes for altitudes above 6,001 feet

16. After processing, turn off the heat and take the lid off the canner.

17. Allow to rest for about 5 minutes before taking the jars out of the hot water.

18. Place the jars on a thick kitchen towel and allow them to cool down for up to 24 hours.

19. Remove the jars, check the seals, label, and store.

Dandelion Jelly

Have you ever tried eating dandelions? This is a unique recipe that uses the lovely flower to make a jelly that will brighten up your bread and pastries.

Time: 40 minutes (steeping time not included)

Serving Size: 3-pint jars

Prep Time: 30 minutes

Processing Time: 10 minutes

Ingredients:

- 2 tbsp lemon juice (freshly squeezed)
- 4 tbsp fruit pectin
- 4 cups of dandelion petals (rinsed, you can also use 2 cups of packed dandelion petals)
- 4 cups of sugar
- 4 cups of water

Directions:

1. In a pot, add 4 cups of water over medium heat and bring to a boil.
2. Take the pot off the heat and add the dandelion petals. Allow the petals to steep for a minimum of 1 hour up to 24 hours.
3. After steeping the petals, pour them into a fine mesh strainer placed over a bowl.
4. Squeeze and press the petals to get all of the dandelion liquid.
5. Prepare the jars by heating them up in the water bath canner. Heat up the water in the canner, but not to the point of boiling.
6. In a pot, add the dandelion tea, pectin, and lemon juice over high heat. Stir everything together and bring the mixture to a rolling boil.
7. Add the sugar and mix well until the sugar dissolves. Return the mixture to a rolling boil.
8. Allow to boil for about 1 to 2 minutes, then take the pot off the heat.
9. Use a ladle and a funnel to spoon the jelly into the jars making sure that there is ¼-inch of headspace.
10. Remove the air bubbles and add more jelly as needed.
11. Wipe the rims of the jars clean, then place the seal and ring.
12. Add the jars to the water bath canner, then bring the canner to a boil.
13. Once the water is boiling, cover the water bath canner and process for 10 minutes.
14. After processing, turn off the heat and take the lid off the canner.

15. Allow to rest for about 5 minutes before taking the jars out of the hot water.

16. Place the jars on a thick kitchen towel and allow them to cool down for up to 24 hours.

17. Remove the jars, check the seals, label, and store.

Mint Jelly

Mint jelly goes well with bread and you can even use it to brighten up lamb chops. Here's another simple recipe for you to try.

Time: depends on the processing time

Serving Size: 4-pint jars

Prep Time: 20 minutes

Processing Time: depends on the processing time

Ingredients:

- 4 tbsp pectin (powdered)
- ¼ cup of lemon juice (freshly squeezed)
- 3 cups of mint leaves (fresh, rinsed, chopped finely)
- 4 ½ cups of water
- 7 cups of sugar

Directions:

1. In a saucepan, add the water and mint leaves over medium heat. Stir well and bring the mixture to a boil.
2. Once the mixture starts boiling, take the saucepan off the heat.
3. Use a lid to cover the saucepan and allow to rest for about 10 minutes.
4. After resting, pour the mixture into a fine mesh strainer placed over a bowl.
5. Squeeze and press the leaves to get all of the liquid, then discard the leaves.
6. Prepare the jars by heating them up in the water bath canner. Heat up the water in the canner, but not to the point of boiling.
7. In a pot, add the mint liquid, pectin, and lemon juice over medium heat. Stir everything together and bring the mixture to a boil.
8. Add the sugar and whisk occasionally until the sugar dissolves. Bring the mixture to a rolling boil.
9. Allow to boil for about 1 to 2 minutes, then take the pot off the heat.
10. Take the pot off the heat and use a spoon to remove any foam on the top.
11. Use a ladle and a funnel to spoon the jelly into the jars making sure that there is ¼-inch of headspace.
12. Remove the air bubbles and add more jelly as needed.

13. Wipe the rims of the jars clean, then place the seal and ring.

14. Add the jars to the water bath canner, then bring the canner to a boil.

15. Once the water is boiling, cover the water bath canner and process based on your altitude:

    a) 5 minutes for altitudes between 0 and 1,000 feet

    b) 10 minutes for altitudes between 1,001 and 6,000 feet

    c) 15 minutes for altitudes above 6,001 feet

16. After processing, turn off the heat and take the lid off the canner.

17. Allow to rest for about 5 minutes before taking the jars out of the hot water.

18. Place the jars on a thick kitchen towel and allow them to cool down for up to 24 hours.

19. Remove the jars, check the seals, label, and store.

Spicy Pepper Jelly

This jelly has just the right kick to it as it combines sweet and spicy peppers. Layer it over cheese for a perfect pairing!

Time: 40 minutes

Serving Size: 3-pint jars

Prep Time: 30 minutes

Processing Time: 10 minutes

Ingredients:

- ½ tsp fine sea salt
- 3 tbsp fruit pectin
- 1 cup of honey
- 1 cup of jalapeño pepper (finely chopped)

- 1 ¼ cups of apple cider vinegar
- 2 cups of sugar (preferably organic)
- 4 cups of red, yellow, and green bell peppers (finely chopped)

Directions:

1. Prepare the jars by heating them up in the water bath canner. Heat up the water in the canner, but not to the point of boiling.
2. In a pot, add the apple cider vinegar, bell peppers, and jalapeño pepper over high heat.
3. Gradually add the pectin while stirring gently, then bring the mixture to a boil. Allow to boil for about 1 to 2 minutes.
4. Add the honey and sugar. Stir well until the sugar dissolves, then return the mixture to a rolling boil.
5. Allow to boil for about 3 minutes while stirring constantly.
6. Take the pot off the heat. Stir the salt into the jelly, then use a spoon to remove any foam on the top.
7. Use a ladle and a funnel to spoon the jelly into the jars making sure that there is ¼-inch of headspace.
8. Remove the air bubbles and add more jelly as needed.
9. Wipe the rims of the jars clean, then place the seal and ring.
10. Add the jars to the water bath canner, then bring the canner to a boil.
11. Once the water is boiling, cover the water bath canner and process for 10 minutes.
12. After processing, turn off the heat and take the lid off the canner.
13. Allow to rest for about 5 minutes before taking the jars out of the hot water.
14. Place the jars on a thick kitchen towel and allow them to cool down for up to 24 hours.
15. Remove the jars, check the seals, label, and store.

Watermelon Jelly

This jelly has a very vibrant color and an intense flavor. Whip it up so that you can enjoy the fresh summer flavor no matter what the season.

Time: 40 minutes

Serving Size: 3-pint jars

Prep Time: 30 minutes

Processing Time: 10 minutes

Ingredients:

- ¼ cup of lemon juice (freshly squeezed)
- ⅓ cup of white wine vinegar
- ¾ cup of fruit pectin (liquid)
- 5 cups of sugar
- 6 cups of watermelon (seeds removed, chopped)

Directions:

1. In a food processor, add the watermelon, and process into a purée.
2. Place a fine-mesh sieve on top of a bowl, then cover it with 4 sheets of cheesecloth.
3. Pour the watermelon purée into the sieve. Allow to stand for about 10 minutes or until you get about 2 cups of watermelon juice.
4. Prepare the jars by heating them up in the water bath canner. Heat up the water in the canner, but not to the point of boiling.
5. In a pot, add the watermelon juice, vinegar, sugar, and lemon juice over high heat.
6. Stir everything together and bring the mixture to a boil. Allow to boil for about 1 to 2 minutes while stirring constantly.
7. Add the pectin and continue to boil for about 1 minute while stirring constantly.

8. Take the pot off the heat and use a spoon to remove any foam on the top.

9. Use a ladle and a funnel to spoon the jelly into the jars making sure that there is ¼-inch of headspace.

10. Remove the air bubbles and add more jelly as needed.

11. Wipe the rims of the jars clean, then place the seal and ring.

12. Add the jars to the water bath canner, then bring the canner to a boil.

13. Once the water is boiling, cover the water bath canner and process for 10 minutes.

14. After processing, turn off the heat and take the lid off the canner.

15. Allow to rest for about 5 minutes before taking the jars out of the hot water.

16. Place the jars on a thick kitchen towel and allow them to cool down for up to 24 hours.

17. Remove the jars, check the seals, label, and store.

Chapter 8:

Recipes for Canning Salsas and Sauces

Salsas and sauces make your meals more interesting. You can pair them with different dishes, which means that having these preserves in your pantry is a must! Here are some simply yet scrumptious salsa and sauce recipes for you to start with.

Apple and Peach Salsa

Combining these two fruits creates a stunning salsa that's subtly sweet and flavorful. Serve it with various dishes to add a fresh and bright sweet flavor.

Time: depends on the altitude

Serving Size: 7-pint jars

Prep Time: 30 minutes

Processing Time: depends on the altitude

Ingredients:

- 2 tsp red pepper flakes
- 1 tbsp canning salt
- 4 tbsp mixed pickling spice
- 2 cups of Granny Smith apples (chopped)
- 2 cups of green bell peppers (seeds removed, chopped)
- 2 ¼ cups cider vinegar (preferably 5%)
- 2 ½ cups of yellow onions (diced)

- 3 ¾ cups of packed light brown sugar
- 6 cups of Roma tomatoes (rinsed, peeled, chopped)
- 8 cups of ascorbic acid solution (⅔ tsp of ascorbic acid mixed with 8 cups of water)
- 10 cups of peaches (hard, unripe, chopped)

Directions:

1. In a bowl, add the apples, peaches, and ascorbic acid solution. Mix well and soak the fruits for about 10 minutes.
2. Layer 2 small sheets of cheesecloth and place the pickling spice in the middle.
3. Wrap the pickling spice by bringing the corners of the cheesecloth together, then tie them up with a piece of string. Set aside.
4. In a pot, add the tomatoes, onion, and bell peppers over medium heat.
5. After soaking, discard the liquid, and add the fruits to the pot.
6. Add the spice bag, vinegar, sugar, red pepper flakes, and salt. Stir everything together and bring the mixture to a boil.
7. Once the mixture starts boiling, turn the heat down to low. Allow to simmer for about 30 minutes while stirring occasionally.
8. Prepare the jars by heating them up in the water bath canner. Heat up the water in the canner, but not to the point of boiling.
9. After simmering, use a slotted spoon to take the spice bag out of the pot.
10. Use a ladle and a funnel to spoon the salsa into the jars making sure that there is 1 ¼-inch of headspace.
11. Remove the air bubbles and add more salsa as needed.
12. Wipe the rims of the jars clean, then place the seal and ring.
13. Add the jars to the water bath canner, then bring the canner to a boil.
14. Once the water is boiling, cover the water bath canner and process based on your altitude:
    a) 15 minutes for altitudes between 0 and 1,000 feet

    b) 20 minutes for altitudes between 1,001 and 6,000 feet

    c) 25 minutes for altitudes above 6,001 feet

15. After processing, turn off the heat and take the lid off the canner.

16. Allow to rest for about 5 minutes before taking the jars out of the hot water.

17. Place the jars on a thick kitchen towel and allow them to cool down for up to 24 hours.

18. Remove the jars, check the seals, label, and store.

Classic Tomato Salsa

When it comes to salsa, tomatoes are the most common ingredient used. Here is a simple recipe for you to make classic tomato salsa with some fresh chilies.

Time: depends on the altitude

Serving Size: 5-pint jars

Prep Time: 30 minutes

Processing Time: depends on the altitude

Ingredients:

- ½ tsp cumin (ground)
- 2 tsp oregano (dried)
- 2 tsp salt
- 2 tbsp sugar
- ½ cup cilantro (fresh, loosely packed, chopped)
- 1 cup of Anaheim green chilies (roasted, peeled, chopped)
- 1 cup of apple cider vinegar
- 1 ½ cups of onion (chopped)
- 7 cups of tomatoes (blanched, grilled, or boiled, peeled, chopped)
- 3 cloves of garlic (minced)
- 3 jalapeños (seeds and stems removed, chopped)

Directions:

1. Prepare the jars by heating them up in the water bath canner. Heat up the water in the canner, but not to the point of boiling.

2. In a pot, add all of the ingredients over medium heat. Stir everything together and bring the mixture to a boil.

3. Once the mixture starts to boil, turn the heat down to low. Allow to simmer for about 10 minutes.

4. Use a ladle and a funnel to spoon the salsa into the jars making sure that there is ½-inch of headspace.

5. Remove the air bubbles and add more salsa as needed.

6. Wipe the rims of the jars clean, then place the seal and ring.

7. Add the jars to the water bath canner, then bring the canner to a boil.

8. Once the water is boiling, cover the water bath canner and process based on your altitude:

    a) 15 minutes for altitudes between 0 and 1,000 feet

    b) 20 minutes for altitudes between 1,001 and 6,000 feet

    c) 25 minutes for altitudes above 6,001 feet

9. After processing, turn off the heat and take the lid off the canner.

10. Allow to rest for about 5 minutes before taking the jars out of the hot water.

11. Place the jars on a thick kitchen towel and allow them to cool down for up to 24 hours.

12. Remove the jars, check the seals, label, and store.

Roasted Spicy Salsa

If you like your salsa with a little kick, then this is the perfect recipe for you. It's easy to make and it packs a lot of flavor!

Time: 50 minutes

Serving Size: 6-pint jars

Prep Time: 40 minutes

Processing Time: 10 minutes

Ingredients:

- ½ tsp black pepper (ground)

- 1 ½ tsp chili powder
- 2 tsp cumin (ground)
- 2 ½ tsp espresso powder
- 3 tsp kosher salt
- ½ cup of cilantro (fresh, chopped)
- 1 cup of apple cider vinegar
- 2 ¼ cups of white onions (diced)
- 4 ½ cups of peppers (a combination of green bell peppers, red bell peppers, and jalapeños, rinsed, dried)
- 5 ½ cups of heirloom or regular tomatoes (rinsed, dried)
- 5 ¾ cups of Roma tomatoes (rinsed, dried)
- 5 cloves of garlic

Directions:

1. Set your oven to broil.
2. In a sheet pan, add the tomatoes and peppers, then spread them out in one layer.
3. Place the sheet pan in the oven. Broil the vegetables until their skin starts to blister.
4. Turn the vegetables over and continue broiling until the skins start to blister.
5. Take the sheet pan out of the oven and allow the vegetables to cool down slightly.
6. When the peppers are cool enough to handle, chop them.
7. Prepare the jars by heating them up in the water bath canner. Heat up the water in the canner, but not to the point of boiling.
8. In a blender, add the tomatoes (along with the juices in the sheet pan), garlic, and half of the onions. Blend until you get a relatively smooth texture.

9. In a pot, add the blended vegetables along with the rest of the ingredients over medium heat. Stir everything well and bring the mixture to a boil.

10. Once the mixture starts to boil, turn the heat down to low. Allow to simmer for about 10 minutes while stirring occasionally.

11. Use a ladle and a funnel to spoon the salsa into the jars making sure that there is ½-inch of headspace.

12. Remove the air bubbles and add more salsa as needed.

13. Wipe the rims of the jars clean, then place the seal and ring.

14. Add the jars to the water bath canner, then bring the canner to a boil.

15. Once the water is boiling, cover the water bath canner and process for 15 minutes.

16. After processing, turn off the heat and take the lid off the canner.

17. Allow to rest for about 5 minutes before taking the jars out of the hot water.

18. Place the jars on a thick kitchen towel and allow them to cool down for up to 24 hours.

19. Remove the jars, check the seals, label, and store.

Salsa Verde

Make this mouthwatering salsa using fresh tomatillos and other ingredients. This salsa goes well with various dishes making it a great addition to your prepper pantry.

Time: 50 minutes

Serving Size: 4-pint jars

Prep Time: 35 minutes

Processing Time: 15 minutes

Ingredients:

- 2 tsp smoked Spanish paprika

- 3 tsp kosher salt
- 2 tbsp cumin
- 6 tbsp lime juice (freshly squeezed)
- ⅔ cup of cilantro (fresh, minced)
- 1 cup of white vinegar
- 2 cups of onion (chopped)
- 2 cups of peppers (a combination of green bell peppers, Thai chilies, and jalapeños, chopped)
- 11 cups of tomatillos (husked, cores removed, chopped)
- 12 cloves of garlic (minced)

Directions:

1. Preheat your oven to 500 °F.
2. On a baking sheet, add ¾ of the tomatillos and arrange them in one layer.
3. Place the baking sheet in the oven. Roast the tomatillos for about 20 minutes until slightly charred.
4. After roasting, take the baking sheet out of the oven. Allow the tomatillos to cool down slightly.
5. Prepare the jars by heating them up in the water bath canner. Heat up the water in the canner, but not to the point of boiling.
6. In a food processor, add the peppers and onion. Pulse until roughly chopped.
7. Transfer the chopped vegetables to a pot.
8. Add the raw and roasted tomatillos to the food processor. Pulse for a few seconds until roughly chopped.
9. Add the tomatillos to the pot along with the rest of the ingredients except for the cilantro.
10. Place the pot on the stove over medium heat. Stir everything well and bring the mixture to a boil.

11. Once the mixture starts to boil, turn the heat down to low. Allow to simmer for about 11 minutes.

12. Add the cilantro, mix well, and continue simmering for about 1 minute more.

13. Use a ladle and a funnel to spoon the salsa into the jars making sure that there is ½-inch of headspace.

14. Remove the air bubbles and add more salsa as needed.

15. Wipe the rims of the jars clean, then place the seal and ring.

16. Add the jars to the water bath canner, then bring the canner to a boil.

17. Once the water is boiling, cover the water bath canner and process for 15 minutes.

18. After processing, turn off the heat and take the lid off the canner.

19. Allow to rest for about 5 minutes before taking the jars out of the hot water.

20. Place the jars on a thick kitchen towel and allow them to cool down for up to 24 hours.

21. Remove the jars, check the seals, label, and store.

Sweet Strawberry Salsa

Have you ever tried sweet salsa? This salsa has a gorgeous vibrant color and the perfect combination of sweet, spicy, and fresh flavors.

Time: 50 minutes

Serving Size: 7-pint jars

Prep Time: 30 minutes

Processing Time: 20 minutes

Ingredients:

- 1 tsp sea salt

- ¼ cup of mint (fresh, finely chopped)

- ½ cup of agave sweetener
- ½ cup of cilantro (fresh, chopped)
- ½ cup of green bell pepper (stems and seeds removed, diced)
- ½ cup of lime juice (freshly squeezed)
- ¾ cup of red bell pepper (stems and seeds removed, diced)
- 1 cup of jalapeño (seeds removed, finely chopped)
- 1 cup of red onion (diced)
- 1 ¼ cups of apple cider vinegar
- 1 ¼ cups of Vidalia onions (diced)
- 5 cups of sugar (granulated)
- 12 cups of strawberries (stems removed, chopped)

Directions:

1. Prepare the jars by heating them up in the water bath canner. Heat up the water in the canner, but not to the point of boiling.
2. In a pot, add the sweetener, sugar, and vinegar over medium-high heat. Stir everything together until the sugar dissolves.
3. Add the lime juice, herbs, onions, peppers, and peppers. Stir everything together and bring the mixture to a boil.
4. Allow the mixture to boil for about 5 minutes before taking the pot off the heat.
5. Fold the strawberries into the mixture making sure to coat all of the fruit pieces completely.
6. Use a ladle and a funnel to spoon the salsa into the jars making sure that there is ½-inch of headspace.
7. Remove the air bubbles and add more salsa as needed.
8. Wipe the rims of the jars clean, then place the seal and ring.

9. Add the jars to the water bath canner, then bring the canner to a boil.

10. Once the water is boiling, cover the water bath canner and process for 20 minutes.

11. After processing, turn off the heat and take the lid off the canner.

12. Allow to rest for about 5 minutes before taking the jars out of the hot water.

13. Place the jars on a thick kitchen towel and allow them to cool down for up to 24 hours.

14. Remove the jars, check the seals, label, and store.

Barbeque Sauce

Make your own barbeque sauce at home to enjoy with meat, chicken, and other grilled foods. This is another simple recipe that belongs in your stockpile.

Time: depends on the altitude

Serving Size: 4-pint jars

Prep Time: 3 hours, 15 minutes

Processing Time: depends on the altitude

Ingredients:

- 1 tsp black peppercorns
- 1 tsp hot pepper sauce
- 1 ¼ tsp cayenne pepper
- 1 tbsp canning salt
- 1 tbsp dry mustard
- 1 tbsp paprika
- 1 cup of brown sugar
- 1 ¼ cups of vinegar (preferably 5%)
- 1 ½ cups of red bell peppers (stem and seeds removed, chopped)
- 2 cups of celery (fresh, chopped)
- 2 cups of onions (chopped)
- 16 cups of tomatoes (peeled, cored, chopped)
- 2 cloves of garlic (crushed)
- 2 hot red peppers (stem and seeds removed, chopped)

Directions:

1. In a pot, add the celery, peppers, onions, and tomatoes over medium heat. Mix everything well and cook for about 30 minutes until the vegetables are soft.

2. Transfer the softened vegetables to a blender, then purée until smooth.

3. Pour the mixture back into the pot and cook for about 45 minutes until it reduces by half.

4. Layer 2 small sheets of cheesecloth and place the peppercorns in the middle.

5. Wrap the peppercorns by bringing the corners of the cheesecloth together, then tie them up with a piece of string.

6. Add the bag to the pot along with the rest of the ingredients.

7. Mix everything well and cook for about 1 ½ to 2 hours until the mixture thickens into a sauce. Stir frequently while cooking.

8. Prepare the jars by heating them up in the water bath canner. Heat up the water in the canner, but not to the point of boiling.

9. Use a slotted spoon to remove the bag of peppercorns from the pot of sauce.

10. Use a ladle and a funnel to spoon the sauce into the jars making sure that there is ½-inch of headspace.

11. Remove the air bubbles and add more sauce as needed.

12. Wipe the rims of the jars clean, then place the seal and ring.

13. Add the jars to the water bath canner, then bring the canner to a boil.

14. Once the water is boiling, cover the water bath canner and process based on your altitude:

    a) 20 minutes for altitudes between 0 and 1,000 feet

    b) 25 minutes for altitudes between 1,001 and 3,000 feet

    c) 30 minutes for altitudes between 3,001 and 6,000 feet

    d) 35 minutes for altitudes above 6,001 feet

15. After processing, turn off the heat and take the lid off the canner.

16. Allow to rest for about 5 minutes before taking the jars out of the hot water.

17. Place the jars on a thick kitchen towel and allow them to cool down for up to 24 hours.

18. Remove the jars, check the seals, label, and store.

Chocolate and Raspberry Sauce

Chocolate and raspberries go so well together. In this recipe, you will make a delicious sauce that pairs perfectly with cake, ice cream, and other sweet treats.

Time: 25 minutes

Serving Size: 3-pint jars

Prep Time: 15 minutes

Processing Time: 10 minutes

Ingredients:

- 3 ½ tbsp pectin (powdered)
- 4 tbsp lemon juice (freshly squeezed)
- ½ cup of cocoa powder (unsweetened)
- 4 ½ cups red raspberries (fresh, crushed)
- 6 ¾ cups of sugar (granulated)

Directions:

1. Prepare the jars by heating them up in the water bath canner. Heat up the water in the canner, but not to the point of boiling.
2. In a bowl, add the pectin powder and cocoa. Mix well and set aside.
3. In a saucepan, add the lemon juice and raspberries over medium heat. Mix until well combined.
4. Whisk the cocoa mixture into the raspberry mixture.
5. Turn the heat up to high, then bring the mixture to a rolling boil while stirring frequently.
6. Once the mixture starts boiling, add the sugar.

7. Mix everything together until the sugar dissolves completely, then bring to a rolling boil while stirring frequently.

8. Continue boiling for about 1 minute before removing the saucepan from the heat.

9. Use a spoon to remove any foam on the top.

10. Use a ladle and a funnel to spoon the sauce into the jars making sure that there is ¼-inch of headspace.

11. Remove the air bubbles and add more sauce as needed.

12. Wipe the rims of the jars clean, then place the seal and ring.

13. Add the jars to the water bath canner, then bring the canner to a boil.

14. Once the water is boiling, cover the water bath canner and process for 10 minutes.

15. After processing, turn off the heat and take the lid off the canner.

16. Allow to rest for about 5 minutes before taking the jars out of the hot water.

17. Place the jars on a thick kitchen towel and allow them to cool down for up to 24 hours.

18. Remove the jars, check the seals, label, and store.

Pear Sauce with Vanilla and Caramel

Here is another sweet sauce for you to try. Combining pears with caramel and vanilla results in a smooth and tasty outcome.

Time: 25 minutes

Serving Size: 4-pint jars

Prep Time: 15 minutes

Processing Time: 10 minutes

115

Ingredients:

- 2 tsp sea salt
- 4 tsp vanilla bean paste
- 3 cups of water
- 6 cups of sugar (granulated)
- 9 cups of pears (cored, chopped)

Directions:

1. Prepare the jars by heating them up in the water bath canner. Heat up the water in the canner, but not to the point of boiling.
2. In a blender, add the pears, salt, vanilla bean paste, and ¼ cup of water. Blend until you get a smooth purée.
3. In a saucepan, add the sugar and 1 ½ cups of water over high heat. Stir well and bring the mixture to a boil.
4. Once the mixture starts to boil, turn the heat down to medium-high. Allow to simmer for about 15 to 20 minutes.
5. After simmering, take the pan off the heat. Add the pear purée and mix well.
6. Place the pot back on the heat until you get the desired consistency.
7. Use a ladle and a funnel to spoon the sauce into the jars making sure that there is ¼-inch of headspace.
8. Remove the air bubbles and add more sauce as needed.
9. Wipe the rims of the jars clean, then place the seal and ring.
10. Add the jars to the water bath canner, then bring the canner to a boil.
11. Once the water is boiling, cover the water bath canner and process for 10 minutes.
12. After processing, turn off the heat and take the lid off the canner.
13. Allow to rest for about 5 minutes before taking the jars out of the hot water.

14. Place the jars on a thick kitchen towel and allow them to cool down for up to 24 hours.

15. Remove the jars, check the seals, label, and store.

Pizza Sauce

Nothing beats homemade pizza. Learn how to make this tasty sauce to slather onto your crust before adding all of your favorite toppings.

Time: 2 hours, 25 minutes

Serving Size: 7-pint jars

Prep Time: 2 hours

Processing Time: 25 minutes

Ingredients:

- 2 tsp peppercorns (cracked)
- 2 tsp rosemary (fresh, chopped)
- 2 tsp sea salt
- 2 tbsp basil (fresh, chopped)
- 2 tbsp oregano
- 2 tbsp sugar
- 4 tbsp parsley (fresh, chopped)
- 6 tbsp olive oil
- 7 tbsp lemon juice (freshly squeezed)
- 3 cups of onions (minced)
- 28 ¾ cups of Roma tomatoes (peeled)

- 4 cloves of garlic (minced)

Directions:

1. In a blender, add the tomatoes and purée until smooth.

2. In a stock pot, add the olive oil, onions, and garlic over medium heat. Sauté for about 4 to 5 minutes until tender and translucent.

3. Add the tomato purée and mix well.

4. Add the rest of the ingredients except for the lemon juice. Stir everything together and bring the mixture to a boil.

5. Once the mixture starts to boil, turn the heat down to medium-low. Allow to simmer for about 2 hours while stirring occasionally.

6. Prepare the jars by heating them up in the water bath canner. Heat up the water in the canner, but not to the point of boiling.

7. When the pizza sauce has reached your desired consistency, add 1 tablespoon of lemon juice to each of the jars.

8. Use a ladle and a funnel to spoon the sauce into the jars making sure that there is ½-inch of headspace.

9. Remove the air bubbles and add more sauce as needed.

10. Wipe the rims of the jars clean, then place the seal and ring.

11. Add the jars to the water bath canner, then bring the canner to a boil.

12. Once the water is boiling, cover the water bath canner and process for 25 minutes.

13. After processing, turn off the heat and take the lid off the canner.

14. Allow to rest for about 5 minutes before taking the jars out of the hot water.

15. Place the jars on a thick kitchen towel and allow them to cool down for up to 24 hours.

16. Remove the jars, check the seals, label, and store.

Spicy Pepper Sauce

Use this spicy sauce in tacos, pasta, soup, sandwiches, and anything else you want to add a kick to! It's very tasty and easy to make.

Time: depends on the altitude

Serving Size: 4-pint jars

Prep Time: 50 minutes

Processing Time: depends on the altitude

Ingredients:

- ½ tsp allspice (ground)
- ½ tsp cloves (ground)
- 1 tsp cumin (ground)
- 1 tsp garlic powder
- 1 tsp mustard (ground)
- 1 tsp sea salt
- 1 tsp turmeric (ground)
- 4 tsp sugar
- 1 cup of apple cider vinegar
- 1 cup of onion (chopped)
- 1 cup of white vinegar
- 2 ¼ cups of peppers (a mixture of hot and sweet peppers, sliced)

Directions:

1. In a stockpot, add the white vinegar, apple cider vinegar, cumin, turmeric, allspice, sugar, mustard, clove, salt, sugar, garlic powder, onion, and peppers over medium heat. Stir everything together and bring the mixture to a simmer.

2. Once the mixture starts to simmer, use a lid to cover the stockpot. Allow to simmer for about 20 minutes.

3. Prepare the jars by heating them up in the water bath canner. Heat up the water in the canner, but not to the point of boiling.

4. After simmering, transfer the mixture to a blender. Purée until you get a smooth and thick consistency.

5. Use a ladle and a funnel to spoon the sauce into the jars making sure that there is ¼-inch of headspace.

6. Remove the air bubbles and add more sauce as needed.

7. Wipe the rims of the jars clean, then place the seal and ring.

8. Add the jars to the water bath canner, then bring the canner to a boil.

9. Once the water is boiling, cover the water bath canner and process based on your altitude:

    a) 10 minutes for altitudes between 0 and 1,000 feet

    b) 15 minutes for altitudes between 1,001 and 3,000 feet

    c) 20 minutes for altitudes between 3,001 and 6,000 feet

    d) 25 minutes for altitudes above 6,001 feet

10. After processing, turn off the heat and take the lid off the canner.

11. Allow to rest for about 5 minutes before taking the jars out of the hot water.

12. Place the jars on a thick kitchen towel and allow them to cool down for up to 24 hours.

13. Remove the jars, check the seals, label, and store.

Chapter 9:

Other Canning Recipes to Try

As a beginner in water bath canning, you can experiment with different recipes that have varying levels of complexities. Doing this will make you feel more confident in your canning abilities. In this chapter, you will learn how to make condiments, pie fillings, and more!

Ketchup

Ketchup is a very common condiment that you can use with different dishes. Make your own ketchup at home and add it to your stockpile.

Time: 45 minutes

Serving Size: 3-pint jars

Prep Time: 30 minutes

Processing Time: 15 minutes

Ingredients:

- 1 tsp allspice (ground)
- 1 tsp black pepper (finely ground)
- 1 tsp celery seed
- 1 tsp cinnamon (ground)
- 1 tsp cloves (ground)
- 1 tsp garlic powder
- 2 tsp ginger (fresh, minced)

- 3 tbsp sea salt

- ½ cup of cane sugar (unrefined, you can also use palm sugar)

- 1 ½ cups of apple cider vinegar

- 2 cups of yellow onion (diced)

- 23 cups of plum tomatoes (chopped)

Directions:

1. In a stockpot, add the onions and tomatoes over medium-high heat. Stir the vegetables together and bring the mixture to a boil.

2. Continue boiling while stirring frequently until the juices are reduced by half.

3. Pour the cooked vegetables into a fine mesh sieve placed over a bowl.

4. Use a spoon to mash the vegetables to separate the liquids from the seeds and skins.

5. Prepare the jars by heating them up in the water bath canner. Heat up the water in the canner, but not to the point of boiling.

6. Pour the vegetable liquid back into the stockpot.

7. Add the sugar, vinegar, sea salt, and all of the spices. Stir everything together and bring the mixture to a gentle boil.

8. Continue boiling until you get the desired ketchup consistency.

9. Use a ladle and a funnel to spoon the ketchup into the jars making sure that there is ½-inch of headspace.

10. Remove the air bubbles and add more ketchup as needed.

11. Wipe the rims of the jars clean, then place the seal and ring.

12. Add the jars to the water bath canner, then bring the canner to a boil.

13. Once the water is boiling, cover the water bath canner and process for 15 minutes.

14. After processing, turn off the heat and take the lid off the canner.

15. Allow to rest for about 5 minutes before taking the jars out of the hot water.

16. Place the jars on a thick kitchen towel and allow them to cool down for up to 24 hours.

17. Remove the jars, check the seals, label, and store.

Wholegrain Mustard

While jams and jellies are easy to prepare and you can consume them immediately. But for mustard, you need to wait for at least one month for the flavors to mellow out.

Time: 30 minutes (soaking time not included)

Serving Size: 3-pint jars

Prep Time: 20 minutes

Processing Time: 10 minutes

Ingredients:

- 2 tsp salt
- ½ cup of brown mustard seeds
- ½ cup of yellow mustard seeds
- ⅔ cup of water
- 1 ½ cups of apple cider vinegar

Directions:

1. In a jar with a lid, add all of the ingredients.
2. Mix well and allow to sit overnight for the mustard seeds to rehydrate.
3. The next day, prepare the jars by heating them up in the water bath canner. Heat up the water in the canner, but not to the point of boiling.
4. Pour the contents of the jar into a blender. Blend until you get the desired mustard consistency.
5. Pour the mustard into a saucepan over medium heat to warm it up.
6. Use a ladle and a funnel to spoon the mustard into the jars making sure that there is ½-inch of headspace.
7. Remove the air bubbles and add more mustard as needed.
8. Wipe the rims of the jars clean, then place the seal and ring.
9. Add the jars to the water bath canner, then bring the canner to a boil.
10. Once the water is boiling, cover the water bath canner and process for 10 minutes.
11. After processing, turn off the heat and take the lid off the canner.
12. Allow to rest for about 5 minutes before taking the jars out of the hot water.
13. Place the jars on a thick kitchen towel and allow them to cool down for up to 24 hours.
14. Remove the jars, check the seals, label, and store.

Pickle Relish

Relish is a wonderful condiment as you can use it in salads and other dishes. This recipe gives you a sweet type of relish to add to your prepper pantry.

Time: 35 minutes (soaking time not included)

Serving Size: 6-pint jars

Prep Time: 25 minutes

Processing Time: 10 minutes

Ingredients:

- 1 tbsp celery seed
- 1 tbsp mustard seed
- ¼ cup of salt
- 1 cup of green bell pepper (chopped)
- 1 cup of red bell pepper (chopped)
- 2 cups of apple cider vinegar
- 2 cups of onions (chopped)
- 3 ½ cups of sugar
- 4 cups of cucumbers (chopped)
- Water (for soaking the vegetables)

Directions:

1. In a bowl, add the bell peppers, onions, and cucumbers.
2. Add the salt and enough cold water to submerge the vegetables completely.
3. Soak the vegetables for about 2 hours.

4. After soaking, drain and discard the liquid.

5. Rinse the vegetables and drain well.

6. Prepare the jars by heating them up in the water bath canner. Heat up the water in the canner, but not to the point of boiling.

7. In a saucepan, add the vinegar, sugar, and spices over medium heat. Stir everything together and bring the mixture to a boil.

8. Once the mixture starts to boil, add the vegetables. Mix well and allow to simmer for about 10 minutes.

9. Use a ladle and a funnel to spoon the relish into the jars making sure that there is ¼-inch of headspace.

10. Remove the air bubbles and add more relish as needed.

11. Wipe the rims of the jars clean, then place the seal and ring.

12. Add the jars to the water bath canner, then bring the canner to a boil.

13. Once the water is boiling, cover the water bath canner and process for 10 minutes.

14. After processing, turn off the heat and take the lid off the canner.

15. Allow to rest for about 5 minutes before taking the jars out of the hot water.

16. Place the jars on a thick kitchen towel and allow them to cool down for up to 24 hours.

17. Remove the jars, check the seals, label, and store.

Sweet Corn Relish

This recipe for homemade sweet corn relish will surely tantalize your taste buds. Prepare this unique and interesting relish, then add it to your stockpile.

Time: 45 minutes

Serving Size: 6-pint jars

Prep Time: 30 minutes

Processing Time: 15 minutes

Ingredients:

- 1 tbsp celery seed
- 1 tbsp mustard seed
- 1 tbsp turmeric
- 2 tbsp flour
- 2 tbsp mustard powder
- 2 tbsp salt
- 4 tbsp water
- 1 cup of onion (finely chopped)
- 1 ¼ cups of white sugar
- 1 ¾ cups of celery (finely chopped)
- 4 cups of bell pepper (finely chopped)
- 4 cups of white vinegar (preferably 5%)
- 8 cups of corn kernels
- 1 clove of garlic (minced)

Directions:

1. Prepare the jars by heating them up in the water bath canner. Heat up the water in the canner, but not to the point of boiling.
2. In a pot, add all of the ingredients except for the flour and water over medium heat.
3. Stir everything well and bring the mixture to a boil.
4. Once the mixture starts to boil, turn the heat down to low. Allow to simmer for about 10 minutes while stirring occasionally.

5. In a bowl, add the flour and water. Mix well.

6. Add 2 to 3 tablespoons of the hot mixture into the bowl and stir well.

7. Pour the mixture into the pot and stir well.

8. Allow to simmer for about 5 minutes while stirring frequently.

9. Use a ladle and a funnel to spoon the relish into the jars making sure that there is ½-inch of headspace.

10. Remove the air bubbles and add more relish as needed.

11. Wipe the rims of the jars clean, then place the seal and ring.

12. Add the jars to the water bath canner, then bring the canner to a boil.

13. Once the water is boiling, cover the water bath canner and process for 15 minutes.

14. After processing, turn off the heat and take the lid off the canner.

15. Allow to rest for about 5 minutes before taking the jars out of the hot water.

16. Place the jars on a thick kitchen towel and allow them to cool down for up to 24 hours.

17. Remove the jars, check the seals, label, and store.

Apple Pie Filling

Homemade apple pie is the ultimate comfort food. If you love making apple pie, it's a good idea to stock up on apple pie filling so you always have it ready when needed.

Time: 55 minutes

Serving Size: 7-pint jars

Prep Time: 30 minutes

Processing Time: 25 minutes

Ingredients:

- ½ tsp nutmeg (ground)
- 1 ½ tsp cinnamon (ground)

- ½ cup of lemon juice (freshly squeezed)
- ¾ cup of Clear Jel
- 1 ¼ cups of water
- 2 ½ cups of apple juice
- 2 ¾ cups of sugar
- 4 cups of water
- 12 cups of apples (peeled, cored, sliced, splashed with fresh lemon juice)

Directions:

1. In a pot, add the water over medium heat and bring to a boil.
2. In batches, blanch the sliced apples in the boiling water for about 1 minute.
3. Transfer the blanched apples to a bowl, then cover the bowl to keep the blanched apples warm.
4. Prepare the jars by heating them up in the water bath canner. Heat up the water in the canner, but not to the point of boiling.
5. In a saucepan, add the rest of the ingredients except for the lemon juice. Stir everything together and bring the mixture to a boil.
6. Once the mixture starts to boil, add the lemon juice. Stir well and return the mixture to a boil. Continue boiling for about 1 minute.
7. Add the sliced apples and mix well.
8. Use a ladle and a funnel to spoon the pie filling into the jars making sure that there is 1-inch of headspace.
9. Remove the air bubbles and add more pie filling as needed.
10. Wipe the rims of the jars clean, then place the seal and ring.
11. Add the jars to the water bath canner, then bring the canner to a boil.
12. Once the water is boiling, cover the water bath canner and process for 25 minutes.

13. After processing, turn off the heat and take the lid off the canner.

14. Allow to rest for about 5 minutes before taking the jars out of the hot water.

15. Place the jars on a thick kitchen towel and allow them to cool down for up to 24 hours.

16. Remove the jars, check the seals, label, and store.

Sweet Pecan Pie Filling

Are you a fan of pecan pie? If you are, then this is the perfect recipe for you. It's wonderfully sweet with a lovely crunch from the pecans.

Time: 40 minutes

Serving Size: 4-pint jars

Prep Time: 20 minutes

Processing Time: 20 minutes

Ingredients:

- ½ tsp cinnamon (ground)
- ½ tsp ginger (ground)
- ½ tsp vanilla extract
- ¼ cup of lemon juice (bottled)
- ½ cup of Clear Jel
- 1 cup of light brown sugar
- 2 cups of sugar
- 3 ½ cups of pecan halves
- 4 cups of apple juice (unsweetened)

Directions:

1. Prepare the jars by heating them up in the water bath canner. Heat up the water in the canner, but not to the point of boiling.

2. In a saucepan, add the sugars, apple juice, Clear Jel, vanilla extract, ginger, and cinnamon over medium-high heat.

3. Stir everything together and cook until the mixture starts to bubble and become thicker. Keep whisking until it boils to ensure a smooth consistency.

4. Once the mixture starts to boil, add the lemon juice. Continue boiling for about 1 minute while stirring constantly.

5. Take the saucepan off the heat and fold the pecans into the filling.

6. Use a ladle and a funnel to spoon the pie filling into the jars making sure that there is 1-inch of headspace.

7. Remove the air bubbles and add more pie filling as needed.

8. Wipe the rims of the jars clean, then place the seal and ring.

9. Add the jars to the water bath canner, then bring the canner to a boil.

10. Once the water is boiling, cover the water bath canner and process for 20 minutes.

11. After processing, turn off the heat and take the lid off the canner.

12. Allow to rest for about 5 minutes before taking the jars out of the hot water.

13. Place the jars on a thick kitchen towel and allow them to cool down for up to 24 hours.

14. Remove the jars, check the seals, label, and store.

Date and Banana Chutney

Chutney is a very popular spread in India. There are many ways to make chutney and this is one of the best. It's incredibly tasty and robust!

Time: 2 hours, 10 minutes

Serving Size: 3-pint jars

Prep Time: 2 hours

Processing Time: 10 minutes

Ingredients:

- ½ tsp salt
- 1 tsp curry paste
- ½ cup of raisins (seeded)
- ½ cup of water
- 2 cups of dates (pitted, chopped)
- 2 cups of sugar
- 3 cups of apples (peeled, cored, chopped)
- 3 cups of banana (peeled, thinly sliced)
- 3 cups of cider vinegar (preferably 5%)
- 1 large lemon (zest and juice)
- 1 large orange (zest and juice)

Directions:

1. Prepare the jars by heating them up in the water bath canner. Heat up the water in the canner, but not to the point of boiling.

2. In a pot, add the zest and juice of the orange and lemon over medium heat.

3. Add the water, apples, cider vinegar, curry paste, and water. Stir everything together and bring the mixture to a boil.

4. Once the mixture starts to boil, turn the heat down to low. Allow to simmer for about 5 minutes.

5. Add the sugar, raisins, dates, and bananas. Continue simmering for about 1 hour to 1 ½ hours while stirring every 10 minutes or so until you get the thick consistency of chutney.

6. Use a ladle and a funnel to spoon the chutney into the jars making sure that there is ¼-inch of headspace.

7. Remove the air bubbles and add more chutney as needed.

8. Wipe the rims of the jars clean, then place the seal and ring.

9. Add the jars to the water bath canner, then bring the canner to a boil.

10. Once the water is boiling, cover the water bath canner and process for 10 minutes.

11. After processing, turn off the heat and take the lid off the canner.

12. Allow to rest for about 5 minutes before taking the jars out of the hot water.

13. Place the jars on a thick kitchen towel and allow them to cool down for up to 24 hours.

14. Remove the jars, check the seals, label, and store.

Green Tomato Chutney

Here's another easy chutney recipe for you. It's easy to make this chutney as you don't even have to peel the tomatoes as part of the prep work.

Time: depends on the altitude

Serving Size: 3-pint jars

Prep Time: 50 minutes

Processing Time: depends on the altitude

Ingredients:

- ⅛ tsp cloves (ground)
- ½ tsp allspice (ground)
- 1 tsp fennel seeds
- 1 tsp red pepper flakes
- 1 tsp salt

- 1 tbsp mustard seeds
- 2 tbsp ginger (candied, chopped)
- 1 cup of apple cider vinegar
- 1 cup of golden raisins
- 1 cup of red onion (chopped)
- 1 ¼ cups of brown sugar (packed)
- 7 cups of green tomatoes (cored, chopped)
- A pinch of nutmeg (ground)
- 1 cinnamon stick

Directions:

1. Prepare the jars by heating them up in the water bath canner. Heat up the water in the canner, but not to the point of boiling.
2. In a pot, add all of the ingredients over medium heat. Stir everything together and bring the mixture to a boil.
3. Once the mixture starts to boil, turn the heat down. Cover the pot with a lid and allow to simmer for about 45 minutes.
4. Use a ladle and a funnel to spoon the chutney into the jars making sure that there is ¼-inch of headspace.
5. Remove the air bubbles and add more chutney as needed.
6. Wipe the rims of the jars clean, then place the seal and ring.
7. Add the jars to the water bath canner, then bring the canner to a boil.
8. Once the water is boiling, cover the water bath canner and process for 15 minutes for altitudes below 1,000 feet or 20 minutes for altitudes between 1,001 and 6,000 feet.
9. After processing, turn off the heat and take the lid off the canner.
10. Allow to rest for about 5 minutes before taking the jars out of the hot water.
11. Place the jars on a thick kitchen towel and allow them to cool down for up to 24 hours.

12. Remove the jars, check the seals, label, and store.

Vegetable Juice

This vegetable juice blend is tasty, refreshing, and healthy. Add this juice to your pantry so that you can have a nutrient-dense drink to boost your energy.

Time: 1 hour, 40 minutes

Serving Size: 7-liter jars

Prep Time: 1 hour

Processing Time: 40 minutes

Ingredients:

- 3 cups of mixed vegetables (a combination of peppers, onions, celery, and carrots, washed, peeled, seeded, finely chopped)
- 22 lbs tomatoes (washed, stems and cores removed)
- Lemon juice (bottled, as needed)
- Salt (as needed)

Directions:

1. Prepare the jars by heating them up in the water bath canner. Heat up the water in the canner, but not to the point of boiling.
2. Roughly chop 5 tomatoes and add them to a large pot over high heat.
3. Mash the tomatoes in the pot to release the juices, then bring the mixture to a boil.
4. Once the mixture starts to boil, chop 5 more tomatoes. Add them to the pot and start mashing.
5. Continue chopping, adding, and mashing tomatoes while making sure that the mixture keeps boiling.
6. After adding all of the tomatoes, allow to simmer for about 5 minutes.

7. Add the rest of the vegetables, mix well, and bring back to a simmer.

8. Allow to simmer for about 20 minutes to soften the vegetables.

9. Pour the mixture into a strainer placed over a bowl to remove any seeds and skins.

10. Pour the juice back into the pot, then season with salt.

11. Use a ladle and a funnel to spoon the juice into the jars making sure that there is ½-inch of headspace.

12. Add 2 tablespoons of lemon juice to each of the jars.

13. Remove the air bubbles and add more juice as needed.

14. Wipe the rims of the jars clean, then place the seal and ring.

15. Add the jars to the water bath canner, then bring the canner to a boil.

16. Once the water is boiling, cover the water bath canner and process for 40 minutes.

17. After processing, turn off the heat and take the lid off the canner.

18. Allow to rest for about 5 minutes before taking the jars out of the hot water.

19. Place the jars on a thick kitchen towel and allow them to cool down for up to 24 hours.

20. Remove the jars, check the seals, label, and store.

Sauerkraut

If you enjoy sauerkraut, why don't you make some at home? Here is a simple recipe for you to make a big batch of this healthy fermented dish.

Time: 40 minutes (fermenting time not included)

Serving Size: 18-pint jars

Prep Time: 20 minutes

Processing Time: 20 minutes

Ingredients:

- 1 ⅛ cups of canning salt
- 25 lbs cabbage

Directions:

1. Remove all of the outer leaves of each head of cabbage.
2. Wash the cabbages thoroughly, cut them into quarters, and remove the cores.
3. Use a knife or a shredder to shred the cabbages thinly.
4. In a bowl, add 5 pounds of shredded cabbage along with 3 tablespoons of canning salt.
5. Toss well and leave for about 10 minutes to let the leaves wilt slightly.
6. Firmly pack the cabbage into a clean pickling container. Use a wooden spoon to press down on the cabbage firmly until the juices come out.
7. Repeat the pickling steps for the rest of the cabbage.
8. Use a cheesecloth to cover the cabbage in the pickling jars. Tuck the edges into the insides of the jars to submerge the cabbage in the juices.
9. Each day, use a spoon to discard any scum that forms on the surface. Ferment the cabbage for about 3 to 6 weeks.
10. When ready to can, prepare the jars by heating them up in the water bath canner. Heat up the water in the canner, but not to the point of boiling.
11. In a pot, add the sauerkraut over medium heat, then bring to a simmer.
12. Use a ladle and a funnel to spoon the sauerkraut into the jars making sure that there is ½-inch of headspace.
13. Remove the air bubbles and add more sauerkraut as needed.
14. Wipe the rims of the jars clean, then place the seal and ring.
15. Add the jars to the water bath canner, then bring the canner to a boil.
16. Once the water is boiling, cover the water bath canner and process for 20 minutes.
17. After processing, turn off the heat and take the lid off the canner.

18. Allow to rest for about 5 minutes before taking the jars out of the hot water.

19. Place the jars on a thick kitchen towel and allow them to cool down for up to 24 hours.

20. Remove the jars, check the seals, label, and store.

Chapter 10:

Focusing on Safety

Becoming a canning pro isn't that difficult. The key is to know what you are doing so that you can get the best outcomes. As you learn how to process different types of food using water bath canning, one of the most important things you need to focus on is safety.

Your main purpose for canning is to have nutritious foods stocked in your pantry. But if you discovered that the canned foods you have stored have gone bad upon opening them, you would end up feeling disappointed. And if such a thing happened during an emergency, you might compromise your family's health and safety. Fortunately, you can easily avoid this by learning all about canning safety.

Common Water Bath Canning Mistakes to Avoid

As a beginner, you have a lot to learn about water bath canning. The more you practice, the more familiar you will be with the process. Simple as this process is, there are some common mistakes a lot of beginners make. Making these mistakes could potentially turn you off from the whole experience. Being aware of them can help you be more careful so that your learning journey can go smoothly.

Not Starting With High-Quality Ingredients

The great thing about water bath canning is that you can use it to preserve a wide range of foods to keep in your stockpile. But if you don't start with fresh, high-quality ingredients, you can't expect to get the best results. Before preparing or cooking your ingredients, inspect each of them first. Make sure to remove any ingredients that have signs of bruising, holes, and other imperfections. That way, you will only be filling your jars with the best ingredients.

Using a Water Bath Canner for Foods That Need to Be Pressure Canned

You already know why certain foods cannot be processed in a water bath canner. There is a risk of botulism and other bacteria growing inside the jars, which would then make the contents unsafe to eat. Make sure that the recipe you will follow includes ingredients that can be safely preserved in a water bath canner. If you're looking for recipes online after trying the recipes in this book, you can confirm the processing method either at the beginning of the recipe or near the end. Check first before you start.

Using the Wrong Size of Canning Jars

Water bath canning recipes should include the jar sizes too. Make sure to follow the correct jar sizes based on the recipe. If you don't have the right jar size, you may have to tweak the recipe a bit. Be as precise as possible when doing this. Consider investing in jars of different sizes so that you can preserve different kinds of preserved food to add to your stockpile.

Using Damaged Canning Jars

While it's okay to reuse canning jars, you need to check them first to see if they are still in pristine condition. Never use jars that have any kind of damage as they might break while you process them in the water bath. Even if they don't break during processing, you can't be sure that they will stay sealed when you store them in your pantry. So if you see any nicks or cracks on your jars, don't use them anymore.

Removing Air Bubbles With a Metal Spoon

Removing the air bubbles from your jars is a simple process. However, you shouldn't use a metal spoon to do this. Remember that the jars you fill are heated and in most cases, the contents are hot too. Using a metal spoon might cause the jars to crack, which would render them unsafe. Use the right tool for this purpose and try to do this step gently so you don't crush or mash the contents. It's also important not to skip this step as any bubbles that are trapped inside the jars will add to the headspace, which would then mess up the preservation process.

Not Adding Enough Water to the Pot

In order for the water bath canning process to work correctly, there needs to be enough water in the pot. The jars should be completely submerged in water. The water should be boiling underneath the jars and above them. Make sure that you have enough water in your pot throughout the process. If the processing time is a bit longer, it's a good idea to keep a kettle of boiling water next to your water bath canner so that you can keep adding more as needed.

Not Considering Your Altitude

The altitude might not seem like a big deal when you're cooking, but it does matter when you're preserving food through water bath canning. The reason for the varying processing times is that water boils at different temperatures depending on the altitude. So the higher your altitude is, the longer the processing time should be. If you don't know your altitude, you can find out using an online search. Then you can adjust your processing times accordingly.

Taking the Jars Out of the Canner Right After Processing

As you may notice in all of the recipes in this book, you should wait for five minutes after processing before taking the jars out of the canner. After processing, take the lid off the pot, then allow the jars to cool down for a bit. This helps ensure that the seals stay in place and the contents won't seep out of the jars.

Storing the Jars Without Removing the Rings

It's important to remove the rings from the lids to make sure that your jars have sealed properly. If you don't do this, it might look like your jars are sealed well but when they cool down, the seals will break. After removing the lids and allowing the jars to completely cool down, try to lift the lid to check if it will stay in place.

Not Labeling Your Jars

Labeling your jars is extremely important, especially if you will store them in your prepper pantry. You know the importance of rotating your stocks and being aware of the expiration dates. Writing down the processing dates of your stocks will make it easier to keep track of everything in your pantry. Keep doing this each time you process a new batch of preserves.

As you can see, these mistakes are very easy to rectify. Although many beginners commit these mistakes, you don't have to since you are already aware of them. Now you can focus on learning how to properly use your water bath canner to process different types of food at home.

Essential Safety Tips to Keep in Mind

When done properly, water bath canning is a safe and simple process that yields wonderful results. Now that you know the common mistakes to avoid while water bath canning, let's go through some final safety tips to complete the knowledge you need to start your learning journey:

- When purchasing tools and equipment, focus on quality. Think of these purchases as an investment for your future food security.

- Use the right tools to ensure that you process your foods safely. For instance, use a jar lifter to take the jars out of the canner after processing. If you don't have a jar lifter, you may use a pair of tongs. Use whatever you have at home, but consider purchasing any tools you are lacking, especially if you plan to keep stocking your pantry with home-canned food.

- Before you start the canning process, make sure to have all of your ingredients and tools on hand. Having to search for items in your kitchen may cause delays, which could compromise the final outcome of the process.

- Always check your jars before and after processing. Do this to make sure that they didn't incur any damage during processing.

- As time goes by, keep yourself updated in terms of water bath canning. Over time, this process may evolve, which means that there might be new guidelines you would have to learn to improve and simplify the process even more.

Finally, if you open a jar of home-canned food that has been sitting on the shelf for a number of months and you smell something off, discard the jar and its contents. By keeping all of these safety tips in mind, you can start water bath canning with confidence and enjoy the results when you're done!

Conclusion:

Water Bath Canning Like a Pro

Water bath canning is a simple and easy process. As long as you focus on safety, it will be a sustainable part of your life. From the beginning of this book, you discovered all of the fundamentals of canning using a water bath.

We started by defining what water bath canning is, how it works, and how it differs from other canning methods. You also learned the many benefits of this preservation method to help you understand why it is very popular. We also discussed the possible risks of this process to give you a holistic understanding of water bath canning.

The next chapter presented you with lists of the best and worst foods to preserve through this canning method. Simply put, you can only preserve high-acid foods through water bath canning. Low-acid foods aren't suitable for this method as the process doesn't reach the right temperature to kill various bacteria that cause food spoilage.

Then we moved on to some beginner tips to help you start your canning journey. In Chapter 3, you discovered the basic equipment needed along with the steps on how to start water bath canning. Before moving on to the recipes, you were also presented with valuable information about starting your own prepper pantry and meal planning routine. These topics will help you see the true importance of food preservation through water bath canning.

Chapters 5-9 contained various canning recipes for you to start with. Try these recipes out to learn how truly simple water bath canning is. In the last chapter, you were presented with the common canning mistakes to avoid along with some important safety tips to keep in mind.

Now that you understand how water bath canning works and how to do it, it's time to start planning. Decide which recipes to try first, then go from there. Happy canning!

References

APA Adamant, A. (2018b, July 7). *How to can mango.* Practical Self Reliance. https://practicalselfreliance.com/canning-mango/

Adamant, A. (2018e, December 16). *Canning blackberries.* Practical Self Reliance. https://practicalselfreliance.com/canning-blackberries/

Adamant, A. (2019b, May 28). *Canning asparagus.* Practical Self Reliance. https://practicalselfreliance.com/canning-asparagus/

Adamant, A. (2020a, May 21). *Dandelion jelly.* Practical Self Reliance. https://practicalselfreliance.com/dandelion-jelly/

Adamant, A. (2020c, September 1). *Canning grapes.* Practical Self Reliance. https://practicalselfreliance.com/canning-grapes/

Adamant, A. (2020d, November 5). *12 Common beginner canning mistakes (And how to fix them).* Practical Self Reliance. https://practicalselfreliance.com/beginner-canning-mistakes/

Adamant, A. (2020e, November 23). *Beginners guide to water bath canning.* Practical Self Reliance. https://practicalselfreliance.com/water-bath-canning-beginners/

Adamant, A. (2020g, December 9). *Canning whole cranberries.* Practical Self Reliance. https://practicalselfreliance.com/canning-cranberries/

Adamant, A. (2022b, June 10). *Corn cob jelly.* Creative Canning. https://creativecanning.com/corn-cob-jelly/

Adina. (2020, June 29). *How to preserve raspberries (Canning raspberries).* Where Is My Spoon. https://whereismyspoon.co/how-to-preserve-raspberries-canning-raspberries/

allinajar2012. (2013, April 12). *How does water bath canning work.* All in a Jar. https://allinajar.com/2013/04/12/how-does-water-bath-canning-work/

Almanac. (n.d.-a). *Recipe for pickled green beans.* https://www.almanac.com/recipe/pickled-green-beans

Almanac. (n.d.-b). *Recipe for zucchini marmalade.* https://www.almanac.com/recipe/zucchini-marmalade

Amanda. (2011, September 10). *Canning salsa verde, made with tomatillos.* Heartbeet Kitchen. https://heartbeetkitchen.com/tomatillosalsaverde/

Amanda. (2013, September 12). *Fiery roasted salsa: A canning recipe!* Heartbeet Kitchen. https://heartbeetkitchen.com/fiery-roasted-salsa/

Ames, M. (2019, March 13). *Rules for safe water bath canning.* Countryside. https://www.iamcountryside.com/canning-kitchen/rules-for-safe-water-bath-canning/

Ann. (2022, May 31). *Sweet pickle relish canning recipe.* Premeditated Leftovers. https://premeditatedleftovers.com/recipes-cooking-tips/sweet-pickle-relish-canning-recipe/

Ball Mason Jars. (n.d.). *How to can: A beginner's guide.* https://www.ballmasonjars.com/canning-and-preserving-101.html

Bauer, E. (2022a, June 14). *Salsa recipe for canning {how to can salsa!}.* Simply Recipes. https://www.simplyrecipes.com/recipes/canned_tomato_salsa/

Belk, M. (2013, May 9). *Canning kiwifruit.* Thrifty Fun. https://www.thriftyfun.com/tf/Food_Tips_and_Info/Canning/Canning-Kiwifruit.html

Bir, S. (2022, May 11). *New to canning? Here's what you need to know.* Simply Recipes. https://www.simplyrecipes.com/water-bath-canning-for-beginners-5271744

Bynum, L. (2019, June 6). *The basics of water bath canning.* The Cooking Bride. https://cookingbride.com/kitchen-basics/water-bath-canning/

Canning grapefruit. (n.d.). Ball Mason Jars. https://www.ballmasonjars.com/blog?cid=canning-grapefruit-ballr-canning-recipes

Carter, B. (n.d.). *The preppers pantry: Essentials of emergency food storage.* US Preppers. https://uspreppers.com/the-preppers-pantry-essentials-of-emergency-food-storage/

Cery. (2018, April 23). *Decadent spiced plums {a canning recipe}.* Back to Our Roots. https://www.backtoourroots.net/spiced-plums

Conte, C. (2013, July 25). *When life gives you figs, make fig jam...orange fig jam.* Christina's Cucina. https://www.christinascucina.com/when-life-gives-you-figs-make-fig-jam/

Davis, A. (2018, May 7). *Water bath canning equipment.* Frugal Living NW. https://www.frugallivingnw.com/water-bath-canning-collecting-the-right-equipment/

EatingWell Editors. (2020, August 20). *10 Steps to Water-Bath Canning.* EatingWell. https://www.eatingwell.com/article/15855/10-steps-to-water-bath-canning/

Fikes, T. (2017, April 15). *59 Water bath canning recipes to try today.* Survival Sullivan. https://www.survivalsullivan.com/water-bath-canning-recipes/

Gordon, B. (2021, February). *3 Strategies for successful meal planning.* Eat Right. https://www.eatright.org/food/planning-and-prep/smart-shopping/3-strategies-for-successful-meal-planning

Grey, M. I. (2020, December 14). *Prepper pantry: 20 Essentials to stockpile.* Survival Sullivan. https://www.survivalsullivan.com/prepper-pantry-essentials/

Grow a Good Life. (2022, June 6). *Pickled garlic canning recipe.* https://growagoodlife.com/pickled-garlic/

Haas, S. (2019, January 30). *Meal preppin' in the pantry.* Plan to Eat. https://www.plantoeat.com/blog/2019/01/meal-preppin-pantry-2/

Happy Preppers. (n.d.). *Prepper pantry list.* https://www.happypreppers.com/preppers-pantry.html

Harbour, S. (2022, March 27). *15 Best prepper pantries and tips on stocking your own.* An off Grid Life. https://www.anoffgridlife.com/best-prepper-pantries/

Healthy Canning. (n.d.-a). *Water bath canning theory.* https://www.healthycanning.com/water-bath-canning-theory/

Healthy Canning. (n.d.-b). *Water bath canning: Step by step.* https://www.healthycanning.com/water-bath-canning-step-by-step

Healthy Canning. (2015b, August 18). *Sweet corn relish.* https://www.healthycanning.com/sweet-corn-relish

Healthy Canning. (2016a, January 2). *Marinated Mushrooms.* https://www.healthycanning.com/marinated-mushrooms

Healthy Canning. (2017a, September 1). *Tomato-vegetable juice blend.* https://www.healthycanning.com/tomato-vegetable-juice-blend

Hill, A. (2019, July 8). *How to meal plan: 23 Helpful tips.* Healthline. https://www.healthline.com/nutrition/meal-prep-tips

Hill, B. (2018, September 4). *Pickled carrots with dill and garlic.* Dish "N" the Kitchen. https://dishnthekitchen.com/pickled-carrots-with-dill-and-garlic/

Hobby Farms. (2021, August 12). *What items should you stock in your prepper pantry?* https://www.hobbyfarms.com/what-items-should-you-stock-in-your-prepper-pantry/

Homestead Dreamer. (2016, November 7). *5 Things you should never water bath can.* http://www.homesteaddreamer.com/2016/11/07/5-things-you-should-never-water-bath-can/

J&R Pierce Family Farm. (n.d.). *The ultimate list of what you can (And cannot!) can.* J&R Pierce Family Farm: Official Blog. https://www.jrpiercefamilyfarm.com/2019/08/15/the-ultimate-list-of-what-you-can-and-cannot-can/

Jennifer. (2016, March 5). *Wholegrain mustard - a water bath food preservation recipe.* Vintage Mountain Homestead. https://oneacrevintagehome.com/wholegrain-mustard-canning/

Johnston, C. (2018, July 23). *Canning salted cantaloupe jam.* Wholefully. https://wholefully.com/canning-salted-cantaloupe-jam/

Kazan, S. (2021, September 21). *A step-by-step guide to water bath canning for beginners.* Alphafoodie. https://www.alphafoodie.com/a-step-by-step-guide-to-water-bath-canning-for-beginners/

Lockcuff, M. (2020, March 11). *Beginner's guide to stocking a working prepper pantry.* Adventures of Mel. https://adventuresofmel.com/beginners-guide-to-stocking-a-working-prepper-pantry/

Magyar, C. (2020, July 14). *15 Potentially dangerous canning mistakes & how to avoid them.* Rural Sprout. https://www.ruralsprout.com/canning-mistakes/

Maria. (2019, July 10). *Canning raw pack whole tomatoes - a step by step guide.* She Loves Biscotti. https://www.shelovesbiscotti.com/canning-raw-pack-whole-tomatoes/

McClellan, M. (2018, October 29). *Pear vanilla caramel sauce.* Food in Jars. https://foodinjars.com/recipe/pear-vanilla-caramel-sauce/

Meredith, L. (2020, September 17). *Boiling water bath and pressure canning - when to use which.* The Spruce Eats. https://www.thespruceeats.com/boiling-water-bath-versus-pressure-canning-1327438

Molina, M. (n.d.). *Sauerkraut for canning.* Allrecipes. https://www.allrecipes.com/recipe/21154/sauerkraut-for-canning/

Mountain Feed & Farm Supply. (n.d.-a). *How to make old fashioned ketchup: Preservative and additive free.* https://www.mountainfeed.com/blogs/learn/40577089-how-to-make-old-fashioned-ketchup-preservative-and-additive-free

Mountain Feed & Farm Supply. (n.d.-b). *Our must-have list of canning equipment & supplies.* Https://www.mountainfeed.com/blogs/learn/15522713-our-must-have-list-of-canning-equipment-supplies

National Center for Home Food Preservation. (n.d.-a). *Barbecue sauce.* https://nchfp.uga.edu/how/can_03/bbqsauce.html

National Center for Home Food Preservation. (2003, August). *How do I? Can salsa.* https://nchfp.uga.edu/how/can_salsa/peach_apple_salsa.html

Norman, C. L. (2002). *SP325-A food preservation methods of canning*. https://trace.tennessee.edu/cgi/viewcontent.cgi?article=1004&context=utk_agexfood

Norris, M. (2022, July 10). *How to can apricots - easy canned apricots recipe*. Melissa K. Norris. https://melissaknorris.com/howtocanapricotscanned-apricots-recipe/

Paa, A. (2021, September 9). *Hot pepper jelly recipe (For canning)*. Heartbeet Kitchen. https://heartbeetkitchen.com/hot-pepper-jelly-recipe/

Penn State Extension. (2019, May 13). *Approved canning methods: Types of canners*. https://extension.psu.edu/approved-canning-methods-types-of-canners

Penn State Extension. (2020, August 31). *Foods that are not safe to can*. https://extension.psu.edu/foods-that-are-not-safe-to-can

Peterson, A. (2022, June 2). *Garlicky pickled mixed veggies*. Better Homes & Gardens. https://www.bhg.com/recipe/garlicky-pickled-mixed-veggies/

Peterson, S. (2021a, March 30). *Canning cherries: Great for quick cobblers, pies, or over ice cream!* Simply Canning. https://www.simplycanning.com/canning-cherries/

Peterson, S. (2022, July 14). *Water bath canning with printable checklist. How to use your canner*. SimplyCanning. https://www.simplycanning.com/water-bath-canning/

Phelan, K. (2019, August 29). *4 Canning dangers to be aware of*. Homestead Survival Site. https://homesteadsurvivalsite.com/canning-dangers/

Pierce, R. (2019a, September 21). *How to can pickled onions – the easiest method*. The Homesteading Hippy. https://thehomesteadinghippy.com/canned-pickled-onions/

Pierce, R. (2019b, November 15). *How to can pickled eggplant step by step*. The Homesteading Hippy. https://thehomesteadinghippy.com/canning-pickled-eggplant/

Polanco, J. (2020, March 23). *What is a prepper pantry and why should you consider starting one?* Julie Naturally. https://www.julienaturally.com/what-is-prepper-pantry/

Pressure Canners. (2018, May 12). *The guide to water bath canning*. https://pressurecanners.com/water-bath-canning/

Rachel. (2015, August 19). *Small batch crunchy canned dill pickles*. Simple Seasonal. https://simpleseasonal.com/recipes/specific-audiences/canning/small-batch-crunchy-canned-dill-pickles

Radaich, M. (n.d.). *Mint jelly*. Food Preserving. http://www.foodpreserving.org/2012/09/mint-jelly.html

Road to Reliance. (2022, March 25). *How to start a prepper pantry - a complete guide.* https://roadtoreliance.com/how-to-start-a-prepper-pantry/

Rose, S. (2020, April 23). *What is a prepper pantry and why should you consider starting one?* Rurally Prepping. https://rurallyprepping.com/prepper-pantry/

Sakawsky, A. (2019, July 6). *Water bath canning for beginners.* The House & Homestead. https://thehouseandhomestead.com/water-bath-canning-beginners/

Sarah. (2019, July 2). *Canning peaches {How to can peaches}.* Sustainable Cooks. https://www.sustainablecooks.com/canning-peaches/

SB Canning. (n.d.-a). *Canning mixed fruit - better in a jar!* https://www.sbcanning.com/2013/03/canning-mixed-fruit-better-in-jar.html

SB Canning. (2016, December 9). *Pecan pie filling {canning recipe}.* https://www.cookingwithmaryandfriends.com/2016/12/pecan-pie-filling-canning-recipe.html

SBCanning. (n.d.). *Four recipe Monday - (1st) green tomato Chutney.* https://www.sbcanning.com/2011/08/four-recipe-monday-1st-green-tomato.html

SDSU Extension. (2022, June 30). *Water bathing vs. pressure canning.* https://extension.sdstate.edu/water-bathing-vs-pressure-canning

Shaw, K. (2022a, April 24). *Triple berry jam for canning.* Heart's Content Farmhouse. https://heartscontentfarmhouse.com/triple-berry-jam/

Shaw, K. (2022b, July 15). *Candied jalapeños for canning {recipe + video}.* Heart's Content Farmhouse. https://heartscontentfarmhouse.com/cowboy-candy-for-canning/

Taste of Home Test Kitchen. (n.d.-b). *Watermelon jelly.* Taste of Home. https://www.tasteofhome.com/recipes/watermelon-jelly/

The Grateful Girl Cooks! (2015, January 30). *Chocolate raspberry sundae sauce.* https://www.thegratefulgirlcooks.com/chocolate-raspberry-sundae-sauce/

Thomas, C. (2020a, January 29). *Step by step tutorial for canning meat (Raw rack nethod).* Homesteading Family. https://homesteadingfamily.com/step-by-step-tutorial-for-canning-meat-raw-pack-method/

Thomas, C. (2020b, September 4). *Canning mistakes to avoid (For water bath & pressure canning).* Homesteading Family. https://homesteadingfamily.com/canning-mistakes-to-avoid/

Toney, S. (n.d.). *Mint jelly.* The Free Range Life. http://www.foodpreserving.org/2012/09/mint-jelly.html

Toney, S. (2018a, October 1). *Canning applesauce - super easy homemade applesauce!* The Free Range Life. https://thefreerangelife.com/homemade-applesauce/

Toney, S. (2018b, October 14). *21 Foods you can preserve in a water bath canner (So easy!).* The Free Range Life. https://thefreerangelife.com/foods-water-bath-canner/

Treadaway, A., & Crayton, E. F. (2019, May 21). *Wise methods of canning vegetables.* Alabama Cooperative Extension System. https://www.aces.edu/blog/topics/food-safety/wise-methods-of-canning-vegetables/Troutman, E. (2020, April 9). *The dangers of water bath canning vegetables.* Burke County Center. https://burke.ces.ncsu.edu/2020/04/the-dangers-of-water-bath-canning-vegetables/

University of Georgia. (2019, August). *Preserving food: Jams and jellies.* https://nchfp.uga.edu/publications/uga/uga_jams_jellies.pdf

Victoria. (2022, May 21). *Beginner's guide to water bath canning.* A Modern Homestead. https://www.amodernhomestead.com/homestead-skills-water-bath-canning/

Vinskofski, S. (2020, July 6). *Homemade hot pepper sauce with instructions for canning.* Learning and Yearning. https://learningandyearning.com/hot-pepper-sauce/

Vuković, D. (2019, May 21). *Water bath canning instructions & safety tips.* Primal Survivor. https://www.primalsurvivor.net/water-bath-canning/

Wahome, C. (2021, August 16). *How to can meat and poultry at home.* WebMD. https://www.webmd.com/food-recipes/features/how-to-can-meat-and-poultry-at-home

Welch, S. (2018, September 20). *Apple pie filling.* Dinner at the Zoo. https://www.dinneratthezoo.com/apple-pie-filling/

Wholesome Farmhouse Recipes. (2021, January 14). *Canning old-fashioned pickled beets.* https://wholesomefarmhouserecipes.com/canning-old-fashioned-pickled-beets/

Winger, J. (2014, September 19). *How to can pears without sugar.* The Prairie Homestead. **https://www.theprairiehomestead.com/2014/09/how-to-can-pears-without-sugar.html**

Image References

APA Aceron, E. (2020). *[Meat]*. Unsplash. [Image]. https://unsplash.com/photos/YlAmh_X_SsE

Babali, S. (2021). *Cherries on Red Background.* Unsplash. [Image]. https://unsplash.com/photos/HUih6WfsZzM

Claire, R. (2020). *Top View of Apple Pie*. Pexels. [Image]. https://www.pexels.com/photo/top-view-of-apple-pie-5863603/

Claire, R. (2021). *Person Carrying a Hot Pot*. Pexels. [Image]. https://www.pexels.com/photo/person-carrying-a-hot-pot-6752363/

Elevate. (2018). *[Wholegrain Mustard]*. Unsplash. [Image]. https://unsplash.com/photos/YtzVxO9NFjc

Escu, A. (2021). *[Pot]*. Unsplash. [Image]. https://unsplash.com/photos/ZaVV6TF7R10

Grachev, R. (2020). *[Vegetables]*. Unsplash. [Image]. https://unsplash.com/photos/eygJ8wxgfng

Henderson, G. (2018). *Mellow Yellow*. Unsplash. [Image]. https://unsplash.com/photos/5HqtJT2l9Gw

Hutter, R. (2020). *Time Timer Watch*. Unsplash. [Image]. https://unsplash.com/photos/xLs4XSQmxtE

Klein, D. (2016). *Fresh Tomato Sauce*. Unsplash. [Image]. https://unsplash.com/photos/FzB_512zvP0

Labenord. (2015). *Jams Marmalades Farmers Market Homemade Preserves*. Pixabay. [Image]. https://pixabay.com/photos/jams-marmalades-farmers-market-997593/

Leung, J. (2018). *[No Labels]*. Unsplash. [Image]. https://unsplash.com/photos/19pdhEmwkBU

Meintjes, S. (2020). *Mint, Herb, Herbs*. Unsplash. [Image]. https://unsplash.com/photos/dJ4JgX5I5y8

Pixabay. (2017). *Clear Glass Mason Jars*. Pexels. [Image]. https://www.pexels.com/photo/clear-glass-mason-jars-48817/

Riggs, S. (2022). *[Pickled Carrots]*. Unsplash. [Image]. https://unsplash.com/photos/RhWNvFxZ0Hg

Shimazaki, S. (2020). *Woman Suffering from a Stomach Pain Lying Down on Couch*. Pexels. [Image]. https://www.pexels.com/photo/woman-suffering-from-a-stomach-pain-lying-down-on-couch-5938365/

Shrewsberry, R. (2021). *Old-Fashioned Root Cellar Showing Preserved Food in Glass Jars*. Unsplash. [Image]. https://unsplash.com/photos/bhni1zsPiio

Yahsi, A. (2020). *[Pickling]*. Unsplash. [Image]. https://unsplash.com/photos/4rPoNLW_3rs

Z Grills Australia. (2020). *Brushing BBQ Sauce on Racks of Ribs in a Z Grill Pellet Smoker*. Unsplash. [Image]. https://unsplash.com/photos/pZyDC7BVN7s

Zolotova, J. (2021). *[Fruits]*. Unsplash. [Image]. https://unsplash.com/photos/M_xIaxQE3Ms

Made in the USA
Monee, IL
08 September 2023